C++ Programming:
A Student-Friendly Approach

Anthony J. Dos Reis

C++ Programming:
A Student-Friendly Approach
Copyright © 2024 by Anthony J. Dos Reis
All rights reserved

ISBN: 9798321374788

TABLE OF CONTENTS

Preface

The objective of this book is to provide the reader with an inexpensive, short, and easy-to-read introduction to C++ and object-oriented programming. It assumes that the reader knows how to program using C. If you do not know C or need a quick review, I recommend *C Programming: A Student-Friendly Approach*. It is inexpensive, short, and easy to read. Its chapters on recursion and linked lists are especially valuable.

This is the second book in a seven-book series on foundational computer science. The objective of the series is to provide the reader with a strong foundation in computer science. With such a foundation, you can more quickly learn, progress, and excel in new areas. You won't need a professor to spoon feed you every new concept. Indeed, you might become the professor. The seven books in the series are

1) *C Programming: A Student-Friendly Approach*
2) *C++ Programming: A Student-Friendly Approach* (this book)
3) *C and C++ Under the Hood 2nd Edition*
4) *Writing Interpreters and Compilers for the Raspberry Pi Using Python 2nd Edition*
5) *Constructing a Microprogrammed Computer 2nd Edition*
6) *Java Programming: A Student-Friendly Approach*
7) *RISC-V Assembly Language*

With the exception of this book (which requires prior knowledge of C), they all have no prerequisites.

The software package for the book is available as a free download. To get the package, send an email to VeniVidiVictusSum@gmail.com. You will immediately get a reply with the link to the software package for this book as well as for the software package for *C Programming: A Student-Friendly Approach*. The package for this book contains files for all the C++ programs that appear in the book, plenty of homework problems, slides, and instructions on using compilers, text editors, and the command line. For each C++ program there are two files: one ready to be compiled, the other with line numbers for use in a classroom presentation. The package also contains the C++ source code for the look program—a program that allows the reader to examine the "insides" of text and binary files.

To report errors or to make comments on this book, please send an email to dosreist@newpaltz.edu.

Anthony J. Dos Reis
Professor Emeritus, Computer Science, SUNY New Paltz

Math Function Summary

To use any of the following functions, include the header file `cmath` in your C++ program (see also `Cfunctions.pdf`).

```
double fabs(double x);
```
       Returns the absolute value of x.
```
double fmax(double x, double y)
```
       Returns the larger of x and y.
```
double fmin(double x, double y)+
```
       Returns the smaller of x and y.

Max, Min, and Absolute Value Functions

```
double cos(double x)
```
       Returns the cosine of x.
```
double sin(double x)
```
       Returns the sine of x.
```
double tan(double x)
```
       Returns the tangent of x.
```
double acos(double x)
```
       Returns the arc cosine of x.
```
double asin(double x)
```
       Returns the arc sine of x.
```
double atan(double x)
```
       Returns the arc tangent of x.

Trigonometric Functions

```
double exp(double x)
```
       Returns e^x.
```
double log(double x)
```
       Returns the natural log of x.
```
double log10(double x)
```
       Returns the base 10 log of x.
```
double pow(double base, double exp)
```
       Returns $base^{exp}$.
```
double sqrt(double x)
```
       Returns the square root of x.

Exponentiation and Log Functions

```
double ceil(double x)
```
       If x is not integral, returns the next integral value > x.
       If x is integral, it returns x.
```
double floor(double x)
```
       Returns the largest integral value <= x.
```
double round(double x)
```
       Returns the integral value nearest to x.
```
double trunc(double x)
```
       Returns the value of x with its fractional part chopped off.

Rounding Functions

1 A Simple C++ Program

Introduction

This book assumes you already know how to program in C. If not or if you need a quick review, we recommend *C Programming: A Student-Friendly Approach*. It is short and inexpensive. But most important, it teaches you not only the principal features of C but also the subtleties of C that are essential to truly "know" C. You may find that the chapters on arrays, recursion, and linked lists extend your understanding of those topics even if you are an experienced C programmer.

We use the **g++** C++ compiler, although you can use any C++ compiler available to you. For instructions on installing and using the **g++** compiler, see `gettingStarted.pdf` in the software package for this book.

C is essentially a subset of C++. Thus, with a few exceptions, a C program is also a C++ program. For example, the following statement is legal in C but not in C++:

```
int *p = malloc(100*sizeof(int));        // cast not required in C
```

In C, the **void** pointer returned by **malloc** is automatically converted to an **int** pointer. But this statement is illegal in C++. We have to explicitly cast the **void** pointer to an **int** pointer in C++:

```
int *p = (int *)malloc(100*sizeof(int));   // cast required in C++
```

In C, a string constant is treated as a pointer to the first character of the string. Thus, it is treated as a **char** pointer. For example, the following statement in C assigns to **p** the **char** pointer that points to the letter "h" in "hello":

```
char *p = "hello";              (cast not required in C)
```

But in C++ we have to write this statement with a cast:

```
char *p = (char *)"hello";      (cast required in C++)
```

In C++, a function whose parameter list is empty is equivalent to an identical function but with **void** in its parameter list:

```
int f()                              int f(void)
{                                    {
     ...        in C++, equivalent to      ...
}                                    }
```

Either way, the parameter list indicates that any call of **f** must *not* pass any arguments. But in C, the two versions are not equivalent: An empty parameter list in C indicates that the function can be called with *any* argument list—that is, with no arguments, with one argument, with two arguments, as so on. But if `void` is specified, the function is equivalent to either C++ version. That is, it cannot be passed any arguments in a call.

For struct and enum declarations, C++ relaxes the requirements that are in C. For example, suppose we declare a struct and an enum with

```
struct S
{
    int x,y;
};
enum Months {Jan=1, Feb, Mar, Apr, May, Jun, Jul, Aug, Sep, Oct, Nov, Dec};
```

Then to declare `s` as a struct and `m` as an enum, we have to include the words "`struct`" and "`enum`", respectively, in their declarations:

```
struct S s;      // "struct" required in C but not in C++
enum Months m;   // "enum" required in C but not in C++
```

But in C++, we can simply use

```
S s;
Months m;
```

g++ *Compiler*

The `g++` compiler consists of four components (see Fig. 1.1): the preprocessor, the translator, the assembler, and the linker. The preprocessor modifies the C++ source code that it inputs. For example, in response to an `#include` directive, it inserts the specified header file into the C++ code that it inputs. The translator component then translates the C++ code outputted by the preprocessor to assembly code. **Assembly code** is simply the symbolic form of machine language. The **assembler** then translates the assembly code to machine language. **Machine language** is the only form of instruction that the computer hardware can directly execute. Finally, the linker combines the output of the assembler with startup code and any functions (obtained from the **C++ Standard Library**) required by the program, all of which are in machine code. **Startup code** is the machine code that gets control first from the operating system when a program is invoked. It performs the initialization required for C++ programs, after which it calls the `main` function.

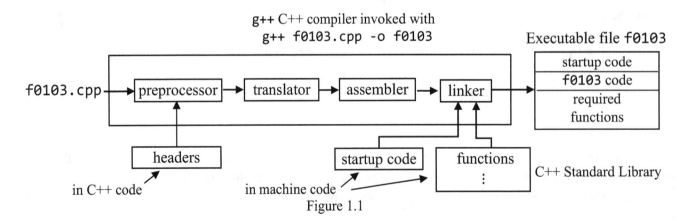

Figure 1.1

Different types of computer systems have different machine and assembly languages. For example, the machine and assembly language for an IBM mainframe is completely different from the machine and assembly language for your personal computer. Fig. 1.2 shows a C++ function along with its corresponding assembly and machine code for the LCC system (the computer system studied in *C and C++ Under the Hood*). Note that there is a one-to-one correspondence between the assembly instructions and the machine instructions. Each assembly instruction is simply a symbolic form of its corresponding machine instruction. In the assembly code, we use easy-to-remember names for the operations to be performed and for the registers (a **register** is a storage area within the CPU that can hold one number). For example, in the add instruction in Fig. 1.2 (add r0, r0, 1), the word "add" is the name for the operation and "r0" is the name for the register that holds one of the numbers to be added. This add instructions adds the value in r0 and 1 and stores the result into r0. The ldr (load register) instruction that precedes the add instruction loads r0 with the value in x. The str (store register) instruction that follows the add instruction stores the result of the add (which is in r0) back into x. Note that the function in the assembly version starts with a label that includes the name of the function followed by the push lr instruction, and ends with the pop lr, ret sequence. The push lr instruction saves the **return address** (the address the function should return to when it is finished) in the lr register. The pop lr instruction at the end restores lr with the return address. Then the ret instruction triggers the return to the return address in the lr.

Machine Code		Assembly Code	C++ Code
1010 1110 0000 0000	@f$i:	push lr	void f(int x)
1010 1010 0000 0000		push fp	{
1010 1011 1000 1100		mov fp, sp	
0110 0001 0100 0010		ldr r0, fp, 2	x++;
0001 0000 0010 0001		add r0, r0, 1	
0111 0001 0100 0010		str r0, fp, 2	
1010 1101 0100 1100		mov sp, fp	}
1010 1010 0000 0001		pop fp	
1010 1110 0000 0001		pop lr	
1100 0001 1100 0000		ret	

Figure 1.2

To see the assembly code *for your computer* that g++ generates, use the -S option when you invoke g++. For example, if you invoke g++ with

    g++ -S f0103.cpp

it outputs the file f0103.s which contains the assembly code for your computer corresponding to the C ++ program in f0103.cpp.

To compile f0103.cpp to the executable file f0103.exe (Windows) or f0103 (Mac, Linux, Raspberry Pi), enter on the command line

    g++ f0103.cpp -o f0103

Then invoke the executable file produced by g++ with

f0103   (Windows) or
./f0103   (Mac, Linux, Raspberry Pi)

Moving from C to C++

Fig. 1.3a shows a simple C program (*which is also a legal C++ program*) and the corresponding program written in the typical style used in C++ programs. The key differences are with keyboard input and display output. On line 7 in Fig. 1.3a, the printf statement displays a prompt message. The corresponding statement in the C++ program uses the cout object. cout represents the standard output stream (i.e., the display). Anything "inserted" into cout is appropriately converted and displayed. The operator "<<" is the **insertion operator**. Thus, line 7 in Fig. 1.3b inserts the prompt string into cout. cout responds by displaying the string.

In the C++ program in Fig. 1.3b, we can also use C-type IO functions, such as printf, as long as we include iostream (as we did on line 1) or stdio.h.

```
1 // f0103.c
2 #include <stdio.h>
3 #include <math.h>
4
5 int main(void)
6 {
7     double x;
8     printf("Enter a number\n");
9     scanf("%lf", &x);
10    printf("sq root of %lf = %lf\n",
11           x, sqrt(x));
12    return 0;
13 }
```
(a)

```
1 // f0103.cpp
2 #include <iostream>
3 #include <cmath>
4 using namespace std;
5 int main(void)
6 {
7     double x;
8     cout << "Enter a number\n";
9     cin >> x;
10    cout << "sq root of " << x
11        << " = " << sqrt(x) << endl;
12    return 0;
13 }
```
(b)

Figure 1.3

On line 9 in Fig. 1.3a, scanf reads in a number into x whose type is double. Note that the format specifier for double is %lf. The corresponding statement in the C++ program (line 9) uses cin. cin represents the standard input stream (i.e., the keyboard). The operator ">>" is the **extraction operator**. Line 9 extracts from cin the keyboard input, converts it to its floating-point format, and stores it in x. The cout statement on line10 (continued on line 11) uses multiple insertions operators to output multiple items: the string "sq root of ", the value of x, the string " = ", the square root of x, and the newline character (endl is equivalent to "\n").

To use cin, cout, and endl, we have to include the header file iostream (see line 2 in Fig. 1.3b). The full names of cin, cout, and endl are std::cin, std::cout, and std::endl, respectively. But we do not have to use these full names in the program in Fig. 1.3b because the using directive on line 4 provides the required prefix "std". This using statement makes all the names (there are many) in the std namespace available to your program. If you want to limit this mechanism to just cin, cout, and endl, then replace the using directive on line 4 with

```
using std::cin;
using std::cout;
using std::endl;
```

To use the `sqrt` function in a C++ program, we have to include the header file `cmath` (or `math.h`). For more math functions, see page *vi* that precedes Chapter 1.

For *numeric* and *string* keyboard input, `scanf` skips over any whitespace (i.e., space, newline, tab), if any, that precedes the keyboard entry of a number or a string. But `scanf` does *not* do this for type `char` entries. For example, in the sequence

```
char c;
int x;
scanf("%d", &x);        // enter 5 then hit the Enter key
scanf("%c", &c);        // the newline is stored in c
```

if a number is entered on the keyboard and then the Enter key is hit, the first `scanf` consumes the number entered, leaving in the keyboard buffer the newline character entered when the Enter key was hit. The second `scanf` then reads in this newline character from the keyboard buffer and stores it in `c`. Thus, the first keyboard entry provides the input for both `scanf` calls. Execution pauses only for the first `scanf`. For example, if you enter 5, and then hit the Enter key (which injects the newline character into the keyboard buffer), the first `scanf` reads the 5 into x, leaving in the keyboard buffer the newline character. The second `scanf` then reads the newline character sitting in the keyboard buffer into `c`. The second `scanf` does not cause a pause in execution that would allow the user to enter a character for `c`. However, if you use `cin` instead of `scanf`, you do not have this problem. `cin`, unlike `scanf`, skips over whitespace for `char` inputs. For example, in the sequence

```
cin >> x;   // reads number into x
cin >> c    // reads first non-whitespace character into c
```

suppose in response to the first `cin`, you enter a number and then hit the Enter key. `cin` then reads the number entered into x, leaving the newline character (injected when the Enter key was hit) in the keyboard buffer. The second `cin` reads the first *non-whitespace* character entered after the number is entered. Thus, it skips over the newline character (which is whitespace) in the keyboard buffer. For example, in response to the first `cin`, if 5 is entered, the 5 is stored in x. The second `cin` then pauses execution until a non-whitespace character is entered, which is stored in `c`. If instead, the sequence 5, space, and the letter "a" is entered and then the Enter key is hit, the 5 is stored in x and the letter "a" is stored in `c` (the space following 5 is skipped).

The problem with `scanf` mentioned above often occurs when a program prompts the user for a "y" or "n" answer. If there is any whitespace left over in the keyboard buffer from a previous input, `scanf` will read it instead of giving the user an opportunity to enter "y" or "n". One solution to this problem is to insert a space just before the format specifier `%c` in the `scanf`:

```
scanf(" %c", &c);           // skips over whitespace
```

Then `scanf` will skip over any whitespace and read into `c` the first non-whitespace character.

Congratulations! Because you know C and have read this chapter, you now know how to program in C++. But there is more to learn. So don't stop now.

2 Function Name Overloading

Encoding the Parameter List

In C++ (but not in C), a program can have multiple functions with the same name. We call this feature of C++ **function name overloading**. Functions with the same name must be distinguishable by their parameter lists. Specifically, the parameter list for each function must differ in order, number, or type from every other function that has the same name. For example, a C++ program can have the following five functions all named f:

```
void f()
{
    ⋮
}
void f(int i)
{
    ⋮
}
void f(char c)
{
    ⋮
}
void f(int i, char c)
{
    ⋮
}
void f(char c, int i)
{
    ⋮
}
```

Because the parameter lists for these functions are distinguishable, the compiler can determine from the argument list in a call of f which f function should be called. For example, if the call is

```
f();
```

then obviously this is a call of the first f function above (the one that has no parameters). If, however, the call is

```
f('a', 3);
```

then this is a call of the last f function above—it is the only f function that has a parameter list whose types match the types of the corresponding arguments in the call.

Although multiple functions can have the same name in a C++ program, they cannot have the same names at the assembler level. If they did, there would be multiple identical labels in the assembly language program. For example, if the C++ names of the five f functions above were carried over to the assembler level, we would get the following assembler code:

```
f:          push lr
              ⋮
            ret
f:          push lr
              ⋮
            ret
f:          push lr
              ⋮
            ret
f:          push lr
              ⋮
            ret
f:          push lr
              ⋮
            ret
```

The multiple occurrences of the label f would cause an assembly-time error.

How then should functions at the assembly level be named? Because functions with overloaded names are distinguishable by their parameter lists, if the compiler includes an *encoding of the parameter list* in the name of the function at the assembly level, then each function will have a unique name.

How parameters are encoded is compiler dependent. Here is the parameter coding scheme we use: The name of a function at the assembly level consists of the character "@", the C++ name of the function, the dollar sign, and the parameter list encoded using the following scheme:

```
v:  void
i:  int
s:  short int
l:  long int
L:  long long int
c:  char
b:  bool
f:  float
d:  double
zc: signed char
uc: unsigned char
ui: unsigned int
us: unsigned short int
ul: unsigned long int
uL: unsigned long long int
```

For example, the name of the following function at the assembly level is @f$ic:

```
void f(int i, char c)
{
    ⋮
}
```

It has an `int` and a `char` parameter which are encoded as "ic" in the assembly-level function name. Thus, this function is translated to

```
@f$ic:    push lr
            ⋮
          ret
```

and the following call

```
f(1, '1');
```

is therefore translated to

```
bl @f$ic
```

Mangled function name

`bl` "branches" to the function at the specified label.

We call the modified function names that appear at the assembly level **mangled function name***s*. The names of all the functions in a C++ program are mangled, except for `main`.

If a parameter is a pointer, then it is encoded with "p" followed by the associated type. For example, if the type of a parameter is `int *`, it is encoded with `pi`.

User-defined types are encoded with the name of the type preceded by the number of characters in the type name. For example, suppose a program uses the following user-defined type:

```
struct Point
{
    int x;
    int y;
};
```

Then the mangled name of the function

```
void f(Point p)
{
    ⋮
}
```

is `@f$5Point`. The number 5 precedes the type name `Point` because there are five characters in `Point`. Without this number preceding the user-defined type name, ambiguity can result. For example, suppose a struct is defined as

```
struct i
{
    int x;
    int y;
};
```

Then the mangled name of a function `f` with one parameter of type `i` would be `@f$i`. But this is also the mangled name of a function `f` that has one parameter of type `int`. If, however, the mangled name of the former included the length of the type name—`@f$1i`—then there would be no clash with the latter.

Function name overloading is an example of polymorphism. **Polymorphism** is a feature of a programming language that allows a single name to have multiple meanings, depending on how it is used. Function name overloading allows a single name, such as f, to refer to multiple functions. Another example of polymorphism in C++ is the plus sign. If its operands are numerical, a plus sign means addition. However, if its operands are strings, a plus sign means **concatenation** (i.e., joining two strings to make a single string). For example, in the following code, x and y are concatenated. Thus, the cout instruction displays "polymorphism".

```
string x = "poly";
string y = "morphism";
cout << x + y << endl;      // illustrates polymorphism
```

Using Default Arguments

Suppose we want to define a function getAvg that returns the average of two numbers. If fewer than two arguments are specified in the call, the missing arguments default to 0.0. One way to create the required getAvg function is to use function name overloading. We get

```
double getAvg(double x, double y)      // use if two arguments in the call
{
    return (x+y)/2.0;
}
double getAvg(double x)                // use if one argument in the call
{
    return x/2.0;
}
double getAvg()                        // use if no arguments in the call
{
    return 0.0;
}
```

If two arguments are passed to getAvg, then the first function above is called. If only one argument is passed, then the second function is called. If no arguments are passed, then the third function is called. However, we can more easily provide the same functionality by using **default arguments**. With default arguments, if the call of a function does not provide an argument for a parameter, then the default argument is assigned to that parameter. For example, in the following implementation of getAvg, if the call passes only one argument, then the default value 0.0 is used for the second parameter y:

```
double getAvg(double x = 0.0, double y = 0.0)
{
    return (x+y)/2.0;           default arguments
}
```

Thus, if getAvg is passed only 100.0, then 100.0 is assigned to x, and the default argument 0.0 is assigned to y in which case getAvg returns 50.0:

```
cout << getAvg(100.0) << endl;   // displays 50.0
```

If **getAvg** is not passed any arguments, it uses 0.0 for both **x** and **y**:

```
cout << getAvg() << endl;          // displays 0.0
```

A parameter for which a default argument is specified is called a **default parameter**. If a call of a function passes *n* arguments, those arguments are assigned to the *first n* parameters. Any remaining parameters must be default parameters, or else a compile time error will result.

There two requirements for default arguments and parameters:

1) All default parameters must be specified to the right of any parameters that are not default parameters. Thus, the parameter list in the following function is *illegal*:

```
void f(int a = 1, int b)          // illegal, b has no default arg
{
    . . .
}
```

2) A default argument must be either a constant or a global variable.

3) The default parameters values should be specified in the function prototype if one is given. For example,

```
 1 #include <iostream>
 2 using namespace std;
 3 void f(int x =  1, int y = 2);    // default values in prototype
 4 int main()
 5 {
 6     f(3);                         // 3 is assigned to x parameter
 7 }
 8 void f(int x, int y)              // y assumes default value 2
 9 {
10     cout << x << endl;           // displays 3
11     cout << y << endl;           // displays 2
12 }
```

3 Reference Parameters/Variables and cout

Reference Parameters

Parameters in C are all value parameters. That is, each parameter is assigned the *value* of its corresponding argument. **Pass by address** in C is not a separate parameter passing mechanism. It is just a special case of call by value in which the value of the argument is an address. In C++, however, parameters can be either value parameters or reference parameters. A value parameter receives the value of the corresponding argument in the function call. A **reference parameter**, in a conceptual sense, receives the argument itself—not its value.

   A parameter is identified as a reference parameter by preceding it with an ampersand ("&"). For example, in the following program, the parameter a on line 4 is a reference parameter:

```
 1 // f0301.cpp  C++ reference parameters
 2 #include <iostream>
 3 using namespace std;
 4 void f(int &a)            & indicates a is a
 5 {                         reference parameter
 6    a = a + 1;       // adds 1 to x
 7 }
 8 //===================
 9 int main()
10 {
11    int x = 5;
12    cout << x << endl;    // displays 5
13    f(x);
14    cout << x << endl;    // displays 6
15    return 0;
16 }
```

Figure 3.1

Conceptually speaking, this is how the reference parameter passing mechanism works in the program in Fig. 3.1: When f on line 13 is called, the variable x itself—not its value—is passed to f where it replaces every occurrence of its corresponding parameter a. Thus, when line 6 is executed, it in effect has been temporarily transformed into

```
    x = x + 1;    // where x is the local variable from main
```

Thus, the effect of f is to increment the value in x by 1. But this is just a conceptual description of what happens. *Here is what really happens*: Because x corresponds to a reference parameter in the function call, the compiler generates code in the calling sequence that *passes the address of* x, even though the address operator & does not precede x in the function call. In other words, the function call on line 13 is translated as if it were written as

```
    f(&x);
```

Thus, the parameter **a** receives the address of **x**. For every occurrence of **a** in **f**, the compiler generates code that dereferences the address in **a**, thereby accessing **x**. Specifically, line 6 is translated as if were written as

```
*a = *a + 1;
```

Thus, this program is translated to the *same* assembler code as the C++ program in Fig. 3.2, except for the mangled name for **f**. In the program in Fig. 3.1, the mangled name for **f** is **@f$ri** where **ri** is the encoding for an **int** reference parameter. In the program in Fig. 3.2, the mangled name for **f** is **@f$pi** where **pi** is the encoding for an **int** pointer.

```
 1 // f0302.cpp  Explicitly passing and dereferencing addresses
 2 #include <iostream>
 3 using namespace std;
 4 void f(int *a)
 5 {
 6     *a = *a + 1;            // adds 1 to x
 7 }
 8 //==================
 9 int main()
10 {
11     int x = 5;
12     cout << x << endl;    // displays 5
13     f(&x);
14     cout << x << endl;    // displays 6
15     return 0;
16 }
```

Figure 3.2

The purpose of a reference parameter is simply to *hide from the programmer* the passing of an address in the call and the dereferencing of that address in the called function. Reference parameters can make a program less complicated and therefore easier to understand.

Reference Variables

A **reference variable** is a variable that is an **alias** (i.e., an alternate name) for another variable. For example, if **xr** is a reference variable that is an alias for **x**, then the following is actually an assignment to **x**:

```
xr = 5;
```

The declaration of a reference variable must specify the variable it is an alias for. For example, the following declaration creates the reference variable **xr** that is an alias for **x**:

```
int &xr = x;
```

A reference variable is just a pointer variable that points to the variable for which it is an alias. Thus, the declaration above creates xr pointing to x:

A reference variable is not like a regular pointer variable in three respects:

1. Once created, it cannot be modified. In other words, it is a constant pointer.
2. Wherever a reference variable is used, the compiler automatically generates code that dereferences it. In contrast, a regular pointer is dereferenced only if it is preceded by an asterisk.
3. A reference variable can never have the value NULL.

Controlling cout

To control the number of digits after the decimal point displayed by cout for floating point numbers, copy lines 6, 7, and 8 in Fig. 3.3 into your program. On line 8, replace 2 with the desired number of digits to be displayed after the decimal point.

```
1 // f0303.cpp
2 #include <iostream>  // needed for cout
3 #include <iomanip>   // needed for setw
4 using namespace std;
5 int main()
6 {
7     cout.setf(ios::fixed);
8     cout.setf(ios::showpoint);
9     cout.precision(2);       // display 2 digits after decimal point
10    double x = 1234.555;
11    cout << x << endl;       // displays 1234.56
12    cout << setw(10) << "hello" << setw(10) << "bye" << endl;
13    cout << std::left << setw(10) << "hello" << setw(10) << "bye" << endl;
14    cout << setw(10) << "hello" << setw(10) << "bye" << endl;
15 }
```

On line 12, setw(10) sets the field width of the next item outputted. The items by default are displayed right justified. Line 13 is 12, but with the addition of set::left which specifies left justification as the default. Thus, line 14, which is identical to line 12, also displays "hello" and "bye" left justified. Here is the output displayed by f0303.cpp:

```
1234.56  ◄── two digits following the decimal point (rounded)
     hello       bye ◄── field width is 10, right justified
hello     bye ◄── field width is 10, left justified
hello     bye ◄── field width is 10, left justified
```

4 C++ Objects

Creating Primitive Variables, Structs, and Objects

Variables—variables with primitive types, structs, and objects—can be created by declaration or allocation. We will see in this section that the way a variable is accessed depends on how it is created.

To create an `int` variable, we can simply declare it, in which case it has a name. For example, to create an `int` variable x, we declare it with

```
int x;
```

We can also create an `int` by dynamically allocating it using `malloc`, in which case it does not have a name:

```
int *p = (int*)malloc(sizeof(int));
```

We can access a variable by its name (if has a name). For example, to assign 5 to x, we use an assignment statement with the name x on its left side:

```
x = 5;
```

To access a dynamically allocated `int`, we dereference the pointer that points to it. For example,

```
*p = 5;
```

We can create a struct by declaring it or by dynamically allocating it. For example, suppose the struct S is defined as

```
struct S
{
   int x, y;
};
```

We can then create an S struct variable by declaring it or by allocating it:

```
S s;                             // creating struct by declaring it
S *p = (S *)malloc(sizeof(S));   // creating struct by allocating it
```

If we declare a struct, we access it using its name. For example,

```
s.x = 5;   // access struct using its name and the dot operator
```

If we allocate a struct, we access it by dereferencing the pointer that is pointing to it using the "->" operator:

```
p->x = 5; // access struct by dereferencing its pointer.
```

An **object** is a structure that contains both data and the functions that operate on that data. An object is created from a class. A **class** is a type that specifies the makeup of an object. A class is essentially the *blueprint* for an object. The data fields and the functions in a class are called **members** of the class.

In C++, an object, like structs, can be created with a declaration in which case the object *gets the name* provided by the declaration. The object is then accessed via its name. For example, if Z is a class that specifies the x and y data fields and the functions set and display, then the following declaration creates an object from the Z class named z:

```
Z z; // creates an object named z from the Z class
```

Fig. 4.1 shows the conceptual picture of the object we get from this declaration:

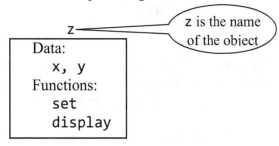

Figure 4.1

Functions and data in a class can be public, private, or protected. If a function or a data member is private, it can be directly accessed *only from within the class*. For example, if x in Fig. 4.1 is private, then it can be accessed only by the set and display functions. If x is public, then it can be accessed from outside the class as well as from inside. public, private, and protected are called **access modifiers** because they determine how object members can be accessed. We will study the protected modifier in the chapter on inheritance. If an access modifier is not specified for a member of a class, it defaults to private access.

If an object *has a name*, we access its public data or invoke its public functions from outside the class using the object's name and the dot operator (just like a struct). For example, line 4 in the following main function assigns 5 to x in the z object (legal only if x is public). Line 5 invokes the set function in the z object, passing it 5 and 6 (legal only if set is public):

```
1 int main()
2 {
3     Z z;
4     z.x = 5;        // using name to access an object
5     z.set(5, 6);    // using name to access an object
6     ...
7 }
```

We have to prefix x and set with the name of the object. If we did not do this, the statements would be ambiguous because there could be other objects with an x variable or a set function.

An object can also be created by allocation using the new operator. For example, the following sequence creates a pointer p and an object from the class Z, and assigns the object's address to p:

```
Z *p;           // declare p as a Z pointer
p = new Z();    // create Z object, assign p the pointer to the object
```

An object created with the new operator *does not have a name*. We access its members via the pointer to it. Fig. 4.2 shows the conceptual picture of the object we get for this example

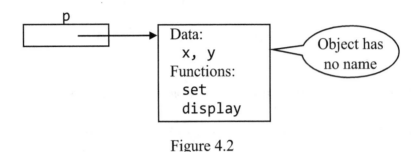

Figure 4.2

Although the object does not have a name, we can access its members via the pointer p using the arrow operator (which consists of a hyphen and the greater than symbol). For example, if set is public, the following statement invokes the set function in the object to which p points:

```
p->set(5, 6);    // using pointer to access an object
```

If x is public, the following statement sets x to 5:

```
p->x = 5;        // using pointer to access an object
```

In C++, we have two ways of accessing an object: via its name (if it has a name) and via a pointer to the object (if we have a pointer that points to the object). Thus, in C++ we need two operators: one for accessing via a name (the dot operator) and one for accessing via a pointer (the arrow operator). But in Java, objects never have names. Thus, in Java, an object in Java is *always* accessed via a **reference** (which is essentially a pointer) to the object. A potential source of confusion for programmers switching from C++ to Java or from Java to C++ is that in Java the dot operator—not the arrow operator as in C++—is used to access an object via a pointer to the object. For example, *in Java*, if p is a reference (i.e., pointer) to an object with a set function, we invoke the set function and pass it 5 and 6 with

```
p.set(5, 6);    // In Java: calling set via pointer p
```

But in C++, this statement would be treated as the call of set in the object whose *name* is p. In C++, to call set via the pointer p, we use

```
p->set(5, 6);    // In C++: calling set via the pointer p
```

Structs Versus Objects

Before we examine a complete C++ program that uses objects, let's examine a program that uses structs instead of objects. We will then compare it with a program that is equivalent but uses objects.

The program in Fig. 4.3 creates structs named a and b on line 24. Because the structs are declared within a function, they are local variables.

```cpp
 1 // f0403.cpp  Using structs
 2 #include <iostream>
 3 using namespace std;
 4 struct S
 5 {
 6    int x;
 7    int y;
 8 };
 9 //===================================
10 void set(S *r, int n, int m)  // r receives the address of the struct
11 {
12    r->x = n;     // dereference r to access x
13    r->y = m;
14 }
15 //===================================
16 void display(S *r)
17 {
18   cout << r->x << endl; // dereference r to access x
19   cout << r->y << endl;
20 }
21 //===================================
22  int main()
23  {
24     S a, b;               // a and b are local structs
25     set(&a, 5, 6);
26     display(&a);          // displays 5 and 6 on separate lines
27     set(&b, 10, 11);
28     display(&b);          // displays 10 and 11 on separate lines
29     return 0;
30  }
```

Figure 4.3

A struct is usually passed to a function by passing the address of the struct rather that its value. Passing the value of a struct creates a parameter which is a complete copy of the struct. If the struct is large, which is commonly the case, creating a copy of the struct is inefficient in both time and space.

Line 24 in Fig. 4.3 creates two type S structs by declaring a and b. The call of the set function on line 25 initializes the x and y fields of the a struct. The calling sequence passes the address of the struct and the values for x and y. The set function dereferences the address it is passed to access the x and y fields of the struct (lines 12, 13). The display function displays the values in the x and y fields. It is passed the address of the struct. Like the set function, it dereferences the address it is passed to access the struct (lines 18, 19). The program then repeats the set and display sequence for the struct b.

The set and display functions work for both the a and b structs (and any other struct of type S). The set and display functions operate on whatever struct whose address they are passed. Thus, to use them on any struct of type S, pass them the address of that struct.

Incidentally, if we rewrite the program above in C, we would have to replace "S" with "struct S" in the declarations that use S. For example, the C++ code on line 24 would have to be changed to

```cpp
struct S a, b;
```

Let's now examine the program in Fig. 4.4. It uses objects in place of the structs in the preceding program. Both programs do the same thing (they both display 5 and 6 and then 10 and 11) but the program in Fig. 4.3 operates on structs and the program in Fig. 4.4 operates on objects.

The class definition is on lines 4 to 12. It specifies what is in an object created from this class. Only the prototypes of the functions appear within the class definition. The definitions of the functions appear after the class definition. The functions are labeled `public`. Thus, they can be invoked from outside the class and well as from inside the class. The x and y fields, however, are labeled `private` so they can be accessed directly only from within the class. Thus, line 33 would be illegal if it were not a comment.

```
 1 // f0404.cpp  Creating objects by declaring them
 2 #include <iostream>
 3 using namespace std;
 4 class Z
 5 {
 6    public:        // public: can be accessed from outside class.
 7        void set(int, int);
 8        void display();
 9    private:       // private: can be accessed only from inside class
10        int x;
11        int y;
12 };
13 //===================================
14 void Z::set(int n, int m)  // Z:: means function is from Z class
15
16    x = n;
17    y = m;
18 }
19 //===================================
20 void Z::display()
21 {
22   cout << x << endl;
23   cout << y << endl;
24 }
25 //===================================
26  int main()
27  {
28      Z a, b;              // a and b are local objects
29      a.set(5, 6);         // passes the address of a, 5, and 6
30      a.display();         // displays 5 and 6 on separate lines
31      b.set(10, 11);       // passes the address of b, 10, and 11
32      b.display();         // displays 10 and 11 on separate lines
33 //   b.x = 20;                illegal if not a comment
34      return 0;
35  }                            Figure 4.4
```

The definitions for the functions in the class are on lines 14 to 18 (the `set` function) and lines 20 to 24 (the `display` function). Note that in the function definitions, the name of each function is qualified with the class name Z (with a double colon separating the class name from the function name). For example, the first line of the `set` function is

```
14 void Z::set(int n, int m)  // Z:: means function is from Z class
```

Its name is prefixed with "`Z::`" (the class name Z followed by a double colon). More than one class in a program can have a `set` function. Thus, the name of a function in its definition must be qualified with the class name to distinguish it from identically named functions in other classes. The double colon between the class name and the function name is called the **scope resolution operator**.

The declaration on line 28 creates two objects: one named a, the other named b. To call a function in an object, we qualify the function name with the object name. For example, to call the `set` function in the a object (legal because `set` is public), we use on line 29

```
29      a.set(5, 6);           // passes the address of a, 5, and 6
```

If x were public, we could access it from outside the class. For example, in `main` we could assign 20 to x in the b object with

```
        b.x = 20;              // illegal because x is private.
```

Fig. 4.5 shows a conceptual picture of the a and b objects created by the preceding program.

Figure 4.5

This conceptual view of the a and b objects leads to two important questions:

1. Each object has its own `set` and `display` functions. Is this not a very inefficient use of memory—to have multiple copies of the `set` and `display` functions?

2. The `set` functions in the a and b objects are *identical*. How then can the `set` functions have a different effect? For example, the call of the `set` function on line 29

    ```
    29      a.set(5, 6);           // passes the address of a, 5, and 6
    ```

    initializes the x and y *in the* a *object*, but the call of the *identical* `set` function on line 31

    ```
    31      b.set(10, 11);         // passes the address of b, 10, and 11
    ```

initializes the x and y *in the* b *object*. Most classes and books on C++ never address this question. Students are simply told that the functions in an object operate on the data *in that object*. Thus, the `set` function in the a object operates on the x and y fields in the a object; the set function in the b object operates on the x and y fields in the b object. Similarly, for the display function. These questions are easily answered by examining the preceding program at the assembly level. At the assembly level, the a and b objects *contain only the x and y data fields—no functions*. Separate from the a and b objects is a *single* set of the set and display functions:

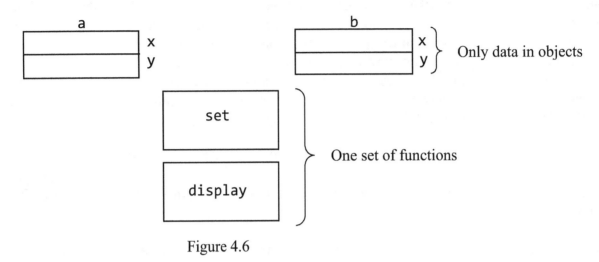

Figure 4.6

Thus, in reality, an object is just a struct that contains *only* the data—none of the functions—associated with the object. Although the conceptual view in Fig. 4.5 does not reflect reality, it nevertheless is an easy way to think of objects and therefore generally is the way most programmers—experienced or inexperienced—think of objects. That is, they think of an object as containing *both* data and functions, and the functions in an object somehow operate on the data in that object. We will follow suit in the upcoming chapters. That is, we will use the conceptual view of objects in our explanations.

Getting back to our two important questions, how then does a single set function have a different effect depending on how it is called? Here is the answer: If it is called with

        a.set(5, 6);

it is passed not only 5 and 6 *but also the address of* a. If it is called with

        b.set(10, 11);

it is passed not only 10 and 11 *but also the address of* b. The set function dereferences the address it is passed to access x and y. Thus, if it is passed the address of a, it sets the x and y in the a object. But if it is passed the address of b, it sets the x and y in the b object. Thus, the set function really has three parameters corresponding to three arguments: the address of the object and the two values inside parentheses in the calling statement. For the call of set on line 29,

```
29      a.set(5, 6);        // passes the address of a, 5, and 6
```

the address of a and the values 5 and 6 are passed to the parameters in the set function. The parameters n and m in the set function,

```
14 void Z::set(int n, int m)  // Z:: means this is set function from Z class
15
16    x = n;
17    y = m;
18 }
```

receive 5 and 6, respectively. The address of **a** is received by a special parameter in the **set** function named **this**. The **set** function dereferences the **this** parameter to access the **x** and **y** variables in the object whose address it is passed. In other words, the compiler treats the **set** function as if it were written this way:

```
void Z::set(int n, int m)
{
   this->x = n; // dereferencing this to access x in object
   this->y = m; // dereferencing this to access y in object
};
```

The same mechanism occurs with the **display** function. The call of **display**,

```
30     a.display();          // displays 5 and 6 on separate lines
```

passes the address of **a**, which is received by the **this** parameter. The **display** function then dereferences the **this** parameter to access the **x** and **y** variables in the object. In other words, the compiler translates the **display** function as if it were written this way:

```
void Z::display()
{
   cout << this->x << endl;
   cout << this->y << endl;
}
```

The most interesting aspect of the programs in Fig. 4.3 and Fig. 4.4 is that at the assembler level, they are *essentially identical*. In Fig. 4.3, line 24 creates the structs **a** and **b**, each with an **x** and **y** field:

```
24     S a, b;              // a and b are local structs
```

But this is precisely what happens on line 28 in Fig. 4.4 that creates two objects:

```
28     Z a, b;              // a and b are local objects
```

The **a** and **b** objects are just structs as we saw in Fig. 4.6. In reality, they do not also contain the **set** and **display** functions (that is just in the conceptual view).

In Fig. 4.3, the call of the **set** function on line 25 passes the address of the struct **a** and the initial values of **x** and **y**:

```
25     set(&a, 5, 6);        // passes the address of a, 5, and 6
```

But this is precisely what happens in the call of the **set** function on line 29 in Fig. 4.4, although it is hidden by the dot notation:

```
29      a.set(5, 6);                // passes the address of a, 5, and 6
```

In the `set` function in Fig. 4.3, `r` is dereferenced to access `x`:

```
12      r->x = n;                   // dereference r to access x
```

where `r` is the parameter that receives the address passed in the call of `set`. Compare that with line 16 in Fig. 4.4:

```
16      x = n;
```

Recall this statement is translated by the compiler as if it were written as

```
        this->x = n;                // dereference this to access x
```

where `this` receives the address passed in the call of `set`. `this` is then dereferenced to access `x`. But this is precisely what happens in the `set` function on line 12 in Fig. 4.3.

Recall from Chapter 3 that reference parameters hide the passing of addresses in the calling sequence and the dereferencing of addresses in the called function. Similarly, the object mechanism hides the passing of addresses in the calling sequence and the dereferencing of addresses in the called function.

A brief digression: If we write the `set` function in Fig. 4.4, prefixing the instance variables `x` and `y` with "`this->`", the name of each parameter can be the same as the name of the instance variable it is initializing. For example, in the following `set` function, we are using the *parameters* `x` and `y` to initialize the `x` and `y` *variables* in the object, respectively.

```
void Z::set(int x, int y)
{
    this->x = x; // left x is instance var, right x is parameter
    this->y = y; // left y is instance var, right y is parameter
};
```

`x` without any prefix refers to the parameter `x`. But `x` with the "`this->`" prefix refers to the `x` variable in the object. Thus, which `x` is being referenced is *not* ambiguous. Many programmers prefer doing this rather than using names for the parameters that do not match the object variables they are initializing.

Creating Structs with malloc and Objects with new

The struct version of the program we examined in the preceding section (Fig. 4.3) creates two structs from the struct `S` with a declaration in `main`:

```
        S a, b;
```

Let's modify `main` so that it creates two structs by allocating them with the `malloc` function. We need two pointer variables to receive the addresses returned by `malloc`:

```
S *p, *q;
```

To dynamically allocate the structs, we use

Cast the `void` pointer returned by `malloc` to `S *`

```
p = (S *)malloc(sizeof(S));
q = (S *)malloc(sizeof(S));
```

`malloc` returns a `void` pointer. We cast the pointer returned by `malloc` so that it matches the type of the p and q pointers. We now have two structs. They *do not have names*, but they have pointers to them. In the program in the preceding section (the struct version in Fig. 4.3), to initialize the a and b structs, we used

```
set(&a, 5, 6);
set(&b, 10, 11);
```

The first parameter is the address of the struct to initialize. In our new version of the program, the addresses of the structs are in p and q. Thus, to initialize the structs, we simply pass set the addresses in p or q and the initial values for x and y:

```
set(p, 5, 6);
set(q, 10, 11);
```

Let's similarly modify the `main` function in the object version of the program we examined in Fig. 4.4. We need two pointers to receive the addresses returned by the `new` operator:

```
Z *p, *q;
```

To dynamically allocate the objects, we use

```
p = new Z(); // the parentheses can be omitted but usually are included
q = new Z();
```

The compiler translates the `new` operator to a call of the `malloc` function. Thus, the assembler code is the same as the assembler code for the struct version that uses `malloc`. In fact, these two statements can be replaced with calls to `malloc`:

```
p = (Z *)malloc(sizeof(Z));
q = (Z *)malloc(sizeof(Z));
```

Recall to access an object via its name, we use the dot operator. But to access an object via a pointer to it, we use the arrow operator. The objects in our new program have no names. But we have pointers to them in p and q. So we use the arrow operator in a call of the `set` function:

```
p->set(5, 6);
q->set(10, 11);
```

The `set` function requires the address of the object when it is called. If the calling statement is

```
        a.set(5, 6);
```

the dot operator indicates that a is the *name* of the object. Thus, the compiler generates code that gets the address of a and passes it to set. But if the calling statement is

```
        p->set(5, 6);
```

the arrow operator indicates that p holds the address of the object. Thus, the compiler generates code that passes the pointer *in* p to set—not the address *of* p. Thus, in both cases, the address of the struct is passed to set. See Fig. 4.7 for the complete program.

```
 1 // f0407.cpp  Creating objects by dynamically allocating them
 2 #include <iostream>
 3 using namespace std;
 4 class Z
 5 {
 6    public:        // public: can be accessed from outside class.
 7         void set(int, int);
 8         void display();
 9    private:      // private: can be accessed only from inside class
10         int x;
11         int y;
12 };
13 //===================================
14 void Z::set(int n, int m)  // Z:: means this is function from Z class
15
11     x = n;
17     y = m;
18 }
19 //===================================
20 void Z::display()
21 {
22     cout << x << endl;
23     cout << y << endl;
24 }
25 //===================================
26 int main()
27 {
28     Z *p, *q;              // a and b are local objects
29     p = new Z();
30     q = new Z();
29     p->set(5, 6);         // passes the address of a, 5, and 6
30     p->display();         // displays 5 and 6 on separate lines
31     q->set(10, 11);       // passes the address of b, 10, and 11
32     q->display();         // displays 10 and 11 on separate lines
34     return 0;
35 }
```

Figure 4.7

The new operator can do more than just allocate objects. For example, it can allocate storage of any type. For example, to allocate an int array with 100 slots, use

```
int *p = new int[100];
```

To allocate a single int, use

```
int *q = new int;
```

Using Constructors

A constructor for a class is a special function that is automatically invoked whenever an object is created from that class. A constructor typically is used to initialize the data in an object. The three characteristics of constructors to remember are

1. The name of a constructor for a class is always the same as the class name.
2. A constructor does not return anything. Thus, it does not have a return type.
3. A constructor for a class is automatically invoked *only* when an object is created from that class.

The name "constructor" is really a misnomer. It is the new operator that constructs (i.e., allocates) the object. The constructor then initializes the object. Perhaps, a better name would have been "initializer". The program in Fig. 4.8 has two constructors. Their prototypes are listed on lines 7 and 8. Note that the name of both constructors (Z) matches the name of the class. The display function prototype listed on line 9 has the return type of void. But no return type appears on lines 7 or 8 for the two constructors.

```
1 // f0408.cpp  Using constructors
2 #include <iostream>
3 using namespace std;
4 class Z
5 {
6    public:
7       Z();        // no parameters, same name as class, no return type
8       Z(int);   // one int parameter, same name as class, no return type
9       void display();
10    private:      // private: can be accessed only from inside class
11       int x;
12 };
13 //===================================
14 Z::Z()
15 {
16    x = 5;        // always initializes x to 5
17 }
18 Z::Z(int i)
19 {
20    x = i;        // initializes x to parameter i
21 }
22 //===================================
```

```
23 void Z::display()
24 {
25    cout << x << endl;
26 }
27 //=================================
28 int main()
29 {
30    Z *p, *q;
31    p = new Z();          // calls constructor that has no parameters
32    p->display();         // displays 5
33    q = new Z(20);        // calls constructor that has single int parameter
34    q->display();         // displays 20
35    return 0;
36 }
```

Figure 4.8

In the program in Fig. 4.8, we are overloading the name of the two constructors—that is, we are using the same name for both constructors (as required by the C++ language). When either constructor is invoked, the argument in the call determines which constructor is called. On line 31, we are invoking the constructor that has no parameters because the call of the constructor has no arguments:

```
31    p = new Z();
```

This constructor initializes x to 5. But on line 33, the call of the constructor has a single int argument:

```
33    q = new Z(20);          // calls constructor that has single int parameter
```

Thus, the constructor with a single int parameter is called which initializes x with the argument 20.
Lines 31 and 33 in Fig. 4.8 create objects from the class Z. We say that lines 31 and 33 **instantiate** (i.e., create) objects. Each object is called an **instance** of the class Z. The data members of each object are called **instance variables** to distinguish them from other types of variables. Instance variables are variables declared *inside* a class. For example, in Fig. 4.8, x is an instance variable, but p and q are local variables in main. A function that is a member of a class is called a **member function**. For example, in Fig. 4.8, display is a member function, but main is not.

Each object created from a class has its own set of instance variables. For example, the program in Fig. 4.8 creates two objects: one on line 31 and one on line 33. Each object has its own x instance variable. The two x variables are distinct. That is, they occupy different locations in memory. As we explained earlier, there is only one set of member functions regardless of the number of objects created from the class. Thus, line 32 and line 34 in Fig. 4.8 both call the *same* display function. However, the two calls have different effects. The call of line 32 affects the x in in the object that p points to; the call on line 34 affects the x in the object q points to. How is this possible, given that both calls are invoking the same display function? The two calls pass different addresses to the display function. Line 32 passes the address in p; line 34 passes the address in q. p points to the x instance variable created by line 31; q points to the x instance variable created by line 33.

Suppose the program in Fig. 4.8 did not have any constructors. That is, suppose lines 7, 8, and 14 to 21 were not present. Then the compiler would translate the program *as if* it had the following constructor, called the **default constructor**:

```
Z()   // default constructor
{
     // empty body so does not initialize x
}
```

The default constructor is what you get if you do not code any constructors in your program. You get the default constructor *only* if you do not code a constructor yourself. Because the default constructor has no parameters, any call of the default constructor has to have no arguments. Thus, with only the default constructor present, line 31 would still be legal (but it would not initialize x)

```
31    p = new Z();    // still legal but does not init x
```

but not line 33 because the call on line 33 has one argument which requires a constructor with one parameter to receive the argument:

```
33    q = new Z(20);  // illegal—no compatible constructor
```

In our example of constructors, we created objects using the new operator. But, as you know, we can also create objects by declaring them. For example, in main in Fig. 4.8, we can also create an object with

```
Z a;          // calls constructor on lines 14 to 17
```

which creates an object with the name a. This declaration *is also a call of a constructor*. In does not specify any arguments. Thus, it calls the constructor that has no parameters on line 14 to 17 which initializes x to 5. When we declare an object, we can specify arguments (within parentheses after the object's name). For example, the declaration

```
Z b(100);     // calls constructor on lines 18 to 21 passing 100
```

specifies the argument 100. Thus, the constructor on lines 18 to 21 is called, which initializes x to 100. If both constructors in Fig. 4.8 were *not* present, then the default constructor would be present. The declaration of a above would still be legal because it is compatible with the default constructor. But the declaration of b would be illegal because there would be no compatible constructor (i.e., a constructor with one parameter).

A function in a class that returns the value of an instance variable is called an **accessor function**. Objects also generally contain one or more **mutator functions**—functions that can modify one or more of the instance variables. The set function in Fig. 4.4 is an example of a mutator function.

Initializing Instance Variables

One way to initialize instance variables is to invoke a member function which is not a constructor that performs the initialization. For example, line 29 in Fig. 4.4 invokes the set function in the a object passing it 5 and 6:

```
29    a.set(5, 6);         // passes the address of a, 5, and 6
```

The set function then initializes the x and y instance variables with 5 and 6, respectively. This approach, however, is *not* a good one because it requires the user to write the code that invokes the function that performs the initialization. The user may not be aware that the object needs to be initialized, or may forget that it needs initialization, or may not know how to do the initialization. Thus, if an object needs to be initialized, it should be done by a constructor, in which case the initialization is performed automatically whenever an object is created. Moreover, a constructor is a function. Thus, it can easily perform complex initializations. For example, if a class has a large array in which each slot needs to be initialized with a random number, it can be done in the constructor with a simple for loop.

If the initialization is simple and the same for every object created from a class, then another acceptable approach is to initialize the instance variables in their declarations. For example, in the Z class in the program in Fig. 4.4, we can specify the initial values of x and y in their declarations:

```
class Z
{
   public:
      void set(int, int);
      void display();
   private:
      int x = 1;        // initialize instance variable x here
      int y = 2;        // initialize instance variable y here
};
```

Encapsulation and Information Hiding

Encapsulation is a mechanism that creates objects. It encapsulates (i.e., binds together) in a single unit both data and the functions that operate on that data. The principal advantage of encapsulation is that it facilitates the sharing of software. Instead of writing all the code for an application, a programmer can simply create objects from pre-written classes. A class has both the data and the functions. Thus, it has everything the programmer that uses the class needs, leaving very little code for the programmer to write.

Instance variables are generally private. Thus, they cannot be accessed directly from outside the class unless it is through a public assessor or mutator function. You can think of the private instance variables in an object as if they are in a protective capsule which allows access only through the provided accessor and mutator functions. Mutator functions are typically written to ensure the integrity of the instance data. For example, a mutator function that updates a test grade stored in an object would check that the grade is within the range of possible grades.

The technique of restricting the access of instance data to accessor and mutator functions is called **information hiding**. In addition to ensuring data integrity, another advantage of information hiding is that it can isolate the implementation of the data from the user of the class. For example, suppose a class has an array that holds a list of numbers. It also has an add function that adds a number to the start of the list. Now suppose the programmer who wrote the class replaces the array with a linked list, and modifies the add function to handle the new implementation. Those modifications do *not* require the program that uses the class to be changed in any way. The program simply calls the add, just like before the modification. Thus, the interface between the user and the object *remains the same* even if the implementation of the data changes.

Using Destructors

A constructor is executed when (and only when) an object is created. A **destructor** is executed when (and only when) an object is destroyed. The name of a destructor includes the class name. But it has the tilde character ("~") as it first character. For example, in Fig. 4.9, Z(int) is the prototype for the constructor (see lines 7 and 13 to 17), and ~Z() is the prototype for the destructor (see line 8 and lines 18 to 22).

```
1 // f0409.cpp  Using destructors
2 #include <iostream>
3 using namespace std;
4 class Z
5 {
6    public:
7        Z(int);    // constructor
8        ~Z();      // destructor, no parameters
9    private:
10       int *p;
11 };
12 //===================================
13 Z::Z(int size)
14 {
15    cout << "in constructor\n";
16    p = new int[size];    // creates array of size int slots
17 }
18 Z::~Z()
19 {
20    cout << "in destructor\n";
21    delete[] p;           // deletes allocated array
22 }
23 //===================================
24 int main()
25 {
26    Z *q;
27    q = new Z(100); // pass argument 100 to size in Z constructor
28    cout << "code that uses q is here\n";
29    cout << "deleting object\n";
30    delete q;        // deletes object but not storage allocated for p
31    cout << "code that does not use q is here\n";
32    return 0;
33 }
```

Figure 4.9

Line 27 in Fig. 4.9 creates a Z object and assigns q the pointer to it.

```
27    q = new Z(100); // pass argument 100 to size in Z constructor
```

The argument 100 is passed to the `size` parameter in the `Z` constructor. The `Z` constructor then allocates an `int` array with 100 slots:

```
16      p = new int[size]; // creates int array of size (100) slots
```

Line 28 represents code that uses the `Z` object created by line 27 via `q` (we omit this code). Using a `delete` statement, line 30 destroys (i.e., deallocates) the object to which `q` points:

```
30      delete q;     // deletes object but not storage allocated for p
```

However, line 30 does *not* deallocate the memory allocated by the `Z` constructor on line 16. But because line 30 deletes (i.e., deallocates) the `Z` object to which `q` points, the destructor is automatically invoked. Line 21 in the destructor then deletes (i.e., deallocates) the storage allocated by line 16:

```
21      delete[] p;  // deletes allocated array
```

Note the use of square brackets on line 21 but not on 29. Why? Line 16, which allocates the memory deallocated by line 21, uses square brackets. So line 21 should also use square brackets as shown. But line 27 does not use square brackets. So line 29 should also not use them.

If the destructor in Fig. 4.9 were not present, the program would have a **memory leak**. That is, it would have memory allocated to it that is no longer accessible and therefore unusable. As an oil leak in a car results in oil the car can no longer use, a memory leak results in memory the computer system can no longer use.

The `cout` statements show the sequence of events as the program in Fig. 4.9 is executed:

```
in constructor            (Z constructor initializes object to which q points)
code that uses q          (code that uses object, not shown in Fig. 4.9)
deleting object           (deleting object invokes destructor)
in destructor             (~Z destructor deallocates memory allocated by constructor)
code that does not use q   (code that does not use object, not shown in Fig. 4.9)
```

You may be wondering why bother deallocating memory during the execution of a program. After all, when a program ends, all its memory is freed up for reuse. To understand why deallocating memory during program execution may be advisable, consider a game-playing program that repeatedly plays games with a user until the user decides to stop playing. If each game requires a large amount of allocated memory, after a few games, there may be no more available memory, in which case the program will crash. If, however, all the allocated memory for that game is deallocated before starting the next game, then there will always be enough memory, no matter how many games the user plays.

Categories of Variables in C++

In C++ there are seven categories of variables:

1) dynamic local variables
2) static local variables
3) parameters
4) global variables
5) static global variables

6) instance variables
7) static class variables

All seven categories are illustrated in the program in Fig. 4.10. Let's start by reviewing the categories we have already encountered (the first six).

A **dynamic local variable** is a variable declared inside a function whose declaration does *not* start with the reserved word `static` (see `dlv` on line 19 in Fig. 4.10). Each time a function is called that has a dynamic local variable, the variable is created. Thus, they are created during runtime ("dynamic" means "during runtime"). A dynamic local variable does not have a specific initial value unless one is specified in its declaration. When the function that contains dynamic local variables ends, its dynamic local variables are destroyed. Thus, the value in a dynamic local variable is not retained from one call of a function to the next. The scope is of a dynamic local variable is local—that is, it is limited to the function in which it is declared.

A **static local variable** is a variable declared inside a function whose declaration starts with the reserved word `static` (see `slv` on line 20). Like a dynamic local variable, its scope is local. But it is created *at compile time*—not at runtime. When the compiler creates an executable file, it includes a slot for each static local variable. Thus, in a sense it exists even before a program starts running. Its initial value is the value specified in its declaration or 0 if no initial value is specified. When a function that contains a static local variable ends, the value in the variable is still there at the beginning of the next call of the same function.

A **parameter** is a variable that receives the value of the corresponding argument in a function call (see `pv` on line 17). It is created when the function is called and destroyed when the function ends. Its scope is local to the function.

A **global variable** is just like a static local variable except that its scope is global—that is, it can be accessed from anywhere in the program (see `gv` on line 4). A global variable is declared outside any functions and classes.

A **static global variable** is just like a global variable except that its scope is limited to the file in which it is declared (see `sgv` on line 5).

An **instance variable** is a variable declared inside a class whose declaration does not start with the reserved word `static` (see `iv` on line 12). Each time an object is created from a class, the object gets a new set of instance variables. For example, the program in Fig. 4.10 creates two objects from the Z class (on lines 35 and 38). Each object has its own `iv` variable. An instance variable in an object retains its value as long as the object remains in existence.

Now let's look at a category of variable that we have not encountered before: a **static class variable** (see `scv` on line 10). A static class variable is a variable declared inside a class (but not inside a function in the class) whose declaration starts with the reserved word `static`. It differs from an instance variable in that there is only one copy regardless of how many objects are created from the class. All the objects created from a class that has a static class variable share the one copy of that variable. A static class variable exists even before any objects are created. Initial values for instance variables take effect when an object is created from that class. Because a static class variable exists even before any objects are created, it must be initialized outside of the class. Line 15, which follows the definition of the Z class, performs this initialization:

```
15 int Z::scv = 40;     // initializing outside of the class
```

Multiple classes might have a static class variable named `scv`. Thus, we have to prefix the variable name with the class name to avoid ambiguity.

```cpp
 1 // f0410.cpp   Types of variables
 2 #include <iostream>
 3 using namespace std;
 4 int gv = 10;             // global variable
 5 static int sgv = 20;     // static global variable (scope limited to file)
 6 class Z
 7 {
 8    public:
 9       void display(int);
10       static int scv;    // static class variable
11    private:
12       int iv = 30;        // instance variable
13 };
14 //===================================
15 int Z::scv = 40;          // must init outside of class
16 //===================================
17 void Z::display(int pv)
18 {
19    int dlv = 50;          // created on each call
20    static int slv = 60; // created at compile time
21    cout << "executing display() in obj " << pv << endl;
22    cout << "pv  = " << pv << endl;
23    cout << "gv  = " << gv << endl;
24    cout << "sgv = " << sgv << endl;
25    cout << "iv  = " << iv << endl;
26    cout << "scv = " << scv << endl;
27    cout << "dlv = " << dlv << endl;
28    cout << "slv = " << slv << endl;
29    gv++; sgv++; iv++; scv++; dlv++; slv++;
30    // final value in dlv lost on exit
31 }
32 //===================================
33 int main()
34 {
35    Z *p, *q;                        // dynamic local variables
36    p = new Z();                     // instantiate object
37    p->display(1);                   // call display() in the object
38    p->display(1);                   // call display() in same object
39    q = new Z();                     // instantiate second object
40    q->display(2);                   // call display() in second object
41    cout << "p   = " << p << endl; // displays address in p
42    cout << "q   = " << q << endl; // displays address in q
43    return 0;
44 }
```

Figure 4.10

The program in Fig. 4.10 produces the following output:

```
executing display() in obj 1
pv  = 1
gv  = 10
sgv = 20
iv  = 30
scv = 40
dlv = 50
slv = 60
executing display() in obj 1
pv  = 2
gv  = 11
sgv = 21
iv  = 31
scv = 41
dlv = 50
slv = 61
executing display() in obj 2
gv  = 12
sgv = 22
iv  = 30
scv = 42
dlv = 50
slv = 62
p   = 0x1f1710
q   = 0x1f1730
```

Not incremented because it is a dynamic local variable

iv in second object so initial value is 30

Addresses in p and q in hex

Note that the second display of the first object shows the values of all the variables are one greater than in the first display, except for `dlv`. This is because `display` increments all the variables each time it is called (see line 28 in Fig. 4.10). `dlv` is an exception because it is a dynamic local variable. Thus, it is created and initialized (to 50) each time `display` is called and destroyed each time `display` returns to its caller. The values of all the other variables are retained between the calls of `display`.

Because a static class variable in a class is shared by all the objects created from that class, it can be used by objects to communicate with each other. One simple application of a static class variable is to keep count of the number of objects in existence. The program in Fig. 4.11 illustrates this technique. Each time an object is created, the constructor increments the static class variable `count`:

```
15 Q::Q()
16 {
17     count++;      // increment when object instantiated
18 }
```

Each time an object is deleted, the destructor decrements `count`:

```
19 Q::~Q()
20 {
21     count--;      // decrement when object deleted
22 }
```

Thus, the value in count is always the number of Q objects that are currently in existence.

```
1  // f0411.cpp  Keeping count of the number of objects
2  #include <iostream>
3  using namespace std;
4  class Q
5  {
6      public:
7          Q();                // constructor
8          ~Q();               // destructor
9          static int count;   // counts number of objects
10         void display();
11     private:
12         int x = 10;
13 };
14 //================================
15 Q::Q()
16 {
17     count++;        // increment when object instantiated
18 }
19 Q::~Q()
20 {
21     count--;        // decrement when object deleted
22 }
23 void Q::display()
24 {
25     cout << "count = " << count << endl;
26 }
27 //================================
28 int Q::count = 0;           // init count to 0
29 //================================
30 int main()
31 {
32     Q *p, *q;
33     p = new Q();     // count incremented
34     p->display();    // count = 1
35     q = new Q();     // count incremented
36     p->display();    // count = 2
37     q->display();    // count = 2
38     delete p;        // count decremented
39     q->display();    // count = 1
40     return 0;
41 }
```

Figure 4.11

When the first object is created on line 33, count is incremented from 0 to 1 by the constructor. count is then incremented to 2 when a second object is created on line 35. When the first object is deleted on line 38, count is decremented back to 1 by the destructor.

5 Copy Constructor

Simple Copy Constructor

A **copy constructor** creates a copy of the object it is passed. The program in Fig. 5.1 does *not* have a copy constructor, nor is one needed. Instead, it simply uses an assignment statement (see line 14) that copies the n object to m.

```
1 // f0501.cpp  Copying an object with an assignment statement
2 #include <iostream>
3 using namespace std;
4 class Z
5 {
6    public:
7        int x = 1; // should be private but public to simplify example
8 };
9 //=====================================
10 int main()
11 {
12    Z n, m;    // create n and m objects with 1 in x variable
13    n.x = 2;   // change x variable in n to 2
14    m = n;     // copies 2 in x variable in n to x variable in m
15    return 0;
16 }                           Figure 5.1
```

Line 12 creates the n and m objects. The x variable in each object contains 1:

Line 13 then changes the x variable in the n object to 2. The assignment statement on line 14 then assigns the n object to the m object. Specifically, it performs a **bitwise copy**—that is, it simply copies all the bits in n to m. Thus, line 14

```
14    m = n;     // copies 2 in x field in n to x field in m
```

copies the 2 in the x variable in n to the x variable in m, resulting in

```
   n                      m
  ┌──────────┐          ┌──────────┐
  │    x     │          │    x     │
  │  ┌────┐  │          │  ┌────┐  │
  │  │ 2  │  │          │  │ 2  │  │
  │  └────┘  │          │  └────┘  │
  └──────────┘          └──────────┘
```

The program in Fig. 5.2 does the same thing as the program in Fig. 5.1, but it uses a copy constructor on lines 16 to 20 to do the copy. For comparison purposes, it also uses an assignment statement to do a second copy operation (see line 32).

```
 1 // f0502.cpp  Copy constructor
 2 #include <iostream>
 3 using namespace std;
 4 class Z
 5 {
 6    public:
 7        Z();    // no-parameter constructor
 8        Z(Z &); // copy constructor uses ref parameter
 9        int x;  // should be private but public to simplify example
10 };
11 Z::Z()
12 {
13    cout << "in no-parameter constructor\n";
14    x = 1;
15 }
16 Z:: Z(Z &original)  // copy constructor
17 {
18    cout << "in copy constructor\n";
19    x = original.x;  // x is in m, original.x is in n
20 }
21 //===================================
22 void display(Z z)
23 {
24    cout << z.x << endl;
25 }
26 //===================================
27 int main()
28 {
29    Z n;          // calls constructor with no parameters
30    Z m(n);       // calls copy constructor, n passed to original
31    n.x++;        // change x in n to 2
32    m = n;        // does not call a constructor
33    display(m);   // calls copy constructor, displays x in m
34 }
```

Figure 5.2

There are two constructors in Fig. 5.2: a constructor that has no parameters (lines 11 to 15) and a copy constructor (lines 16 to 20) that has a single parameter of type Z. Line 29 creates the n object. Because it does not specify any arguments, it calls the constructor on lines 11 to 15 that has no parameters. Line 30 on the other hand specifies the argument n whose type matches the parameter in the copy constructor. Thus, line 30 calls the copy constructor. The ampersand ("&") on the first line of the copy constructor indicates that the parameter `original` is a reference parameter—not a value parameter. Thus, in effect the argument n on line 30 replaces the parameter `original`. Thus, `original.x` on line 19 in effect is n.x.

Line 30 automatically calls the copy constructor in m so the left x on line 19 is the x in m:

```
30    Z m(n);       // calls copy constructor in m, not in n.
```

Thus, line 19 simply copies `original.x` (i.e., the x in n) to the x in m, which is *exactly what the assignment statement* on line 32 does. For this program, we *do not need* the copy constructor. We can use an assignment statement instead.

Both constructors in Fig. 5.2 display a message when executed. When the program is executed, the constructors display the following messages, followed by 2 (from the call of `display` on line 33):

in no-parameter constructor	(called by line 29)
in copy constructor	(called by line 30)
in copy constructor	(called by line 33)
2	(displayed by line 33)

From these messages, we can tell which lines are calling which constructors. Line 29 calls the no-parameter constructor. Line 30 calls the copy constructor. What is particularly interesting is that line 33 *also calls the copy constructor*. It does this because it uses pass by value. Thus, the parameter z is created by *creating a copy* of the argument m. It *is the copy constructor* that does this. Now you can understand why pass by reference (indicated by the "&") is used by the copy constructor. If, instead, we use pass by value, then the creation of the parameter `original` in the copy constructor would trigger another execution of the copy constructor. But that would trigger yet another execution of the copy constructor, and so on. The copy constructor would recursively call itself forever (try deleting the ampersand on line 16 to see what happens when the modified is executed).

Copy Constructor that Handles Pointers

It appears from the programs in Fig. 5.1 and Fig. 5.2, a copy constructor is not needed. We can always use instead an assignment statement to copy objects. However, if we do this, we sometimes run into some problems, as illustrated by the program in Fig. 5.3. What is different about the program in Fig. 5.3 is that the objects it creates *contain pointers*.

```
1 // f0503.cpp  Importance of copy constructors
2 #include <iostream>
3 using namespace std;
4 class Z
5 {
6    public:
7        Z(int x); // constructor
8        ~Z();      // destructor
9    private:
10       int *p;   // int pointer
11 };
12 Z::Z(int x)
13 {
14    p = new int; // allocate int
15    *p = x;      // init to x
16 }
17 Z::~Z()
18 {
19    delete p;    // prevents memory leak
20 }
21 //====================================
22 int main()
23 {
24    Z n(1);       // creates n object with x = 1
25    Z m(2);       // creates m object with x = 2
26    m = n;        // copies object, memory leak
27    return 0;
28 }
```

Figure 5.3

Lines 24 and 25 pass an int value to the parameter x in the constructor on lines 12 to 16. The constructor then allocates memory for an int, assigns its pointer to p, and stores x in the allocated storage. We get

Line 26 then copies the n object to the m object using an assignment statement. The assignment statement simply copies the instance variable p in n to the corresponding instance variable in m. We get

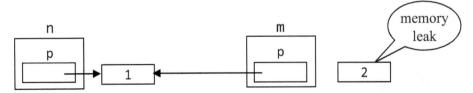

There are four problems with this new configuration:

1) It creates a memory leak. The memory that p in m was pointing to is still allocated but inaccessible, and therefore unusable.
2) If the n object is deleted, its destructor on line 19 also deletes the int that p is pointing to. Thus, the p in m will then point to an int that no longer exists.
3) If n and m are deleted in that order, the destructors in n and m are both executed. Thus, the system will attempt to delete the storage p points to a second time when m is deleted.
4) The n and m objects are not independent. They share the int that their p variables point to. Thus, if the n object modifies the int its p points to, it affects the int that the p in m points to.

When n **is** copied to m, we want n and m to be identical but *completely independent* like so:

To copy objects with pointers so that the copy is completely independent of the original, we have to use a copy constructor which allocates memory in the receiving object and then copies the allocated memory in the original to its allocated memory in the receiving object. The program in Fig. 5.4 illustrates this technique.

Line 31 calls the copy constructor in m, which copies the n object to the m object.

```
31    Z m(n);      // no memory leak, calls copy constructor in m
```

It does *not* copy p in n to the p in m, as an assignment statement would do. Instead, on line 20, it allocates its own memory.

```
20    p = new int;
```

Next, it dereferences `original.p` (which is the p in n) to get the contents of the allocated memory in n, which it then assigns to the memory p points to, where p is the p in m:

```
21    *p = *(original.p);
```

The result is two identical but completely independent objects. Line 32 then repeats the copy, but this time with an assignment statement, which, as we already observed, does not work correctly:

```
32    m = n;       // memory leak and other problems
```

We call a copy that creates two completely independent objects (like the program in Fig. 5.4) a **deep copy**. A copy that does not create two completely independent object because it copies only the instance variables in the original to the instance variables in the copy (like the program in Fig. 5.3) a **shallow copy.**

```
 1 // f0504.cpp   Importance of copy constructors
 2 #include <iostream>
 3 using namespace std;
 4 class Z
 5 {
 6     public:
 7         Z(int x);
 8         Z(Z &);
 9         ~Z();
10     private:
11         int *p;
12 };
13 Z::Z(int x)
14 {
15     p = new int;
16     *p = x;
17 }
18 Z::Z(Z &original)
19 {
20     p = new int;
21     *p = *(original.p);
22 }
23 Z::~Z()
24 {
25     delete p;
26 }
27 //=====================================
28 int main()
29 {
30     Z n(1);        // calls constructor on line 13
31     Z m(n);        // no memory leak, calls copy constructor in m
32     m = n;         // memory leak and other problems
33     return 0;
34 }
```

Figure 5.4

6 Strings and Boolean Variables

Strings in C

In C++, there are two kinds of strings: the kind in C (which are also in C++), and the kind in C++ only. We call the former a **C-type string**, and the latter, a **C++-type string**.

In C, there is no string type. However, we can use a char array in lieu of a string variable. For example, the following *declaration* initializes the a array with the string constant "yes":

```
char a[10] = "yes";   // this is declaration–NOT assignment statement
```

Thus, the first four slots of a will then contain 'y', 'e', 's', '\0'. The null character, '\0', marks the end of the string. It is one byte with all zero bits. However, we *cannot* assign a string to a with an *assignment statement*:

```
a = "yes";            // this is assignment statement--ILLEGAL
```

a, the name of the array without the square brackets, is treated as &a[0]—that is, as the address of the first slot of the a array. a *always* points to the first slot of the a array. It is a *constant* pointer. Thus, the statement above is *illegal* because it attempts to modify a constant pointer. To assign a string to a, use the strcpy function (in C++, include string.h or cstring in the program):

```
strcpy(a, "hello");   // copies "hello" to a array
```

To assign the string in a to a char array b, similarly use the strcpy function:

```
strcpy(b, a);         // copies string in a to b
```

To display the strings in a and b, we can use

```
printf("%s %s\n", a, b);          // in C or C++ program
              or
cout << a << " " << b << endl;    // in C++ program
```

We can also use a char pointer to point to a string. For example, in

```
char *p, *q;
p = (char *)"yes";          // p now points to "y" in "yes"
q = p;                      // q now points to "y" in "yes"
```

the C compiler places the string constant "yes" out of the flow of control (so the CPU will not attempt to execute it as if it were machine instructions). In place of the string constant in the instruction, the compiler uses the address of the first character in the string (i.e., the address of "y" in "yes"). Thus, the first assignment statement above assigns p the address of the string (or more precisely, the address of its first character). The second assignment statement then assigns this address in p to q. Thus, both p and q then point to the same string "yes". Then either of the following statements

```
        printf("%s %s/n", p, q);          // legal in a C or C++ program
        cout << p << " " << q << endl;    // legal only in a C++ program
```

displays

```
yes yes
```

To use the C type string functions like `strcpy` in a C++ program, your C++ program should include

```
#include <cstring>
```
    or
```
#include <string.h>
```

To use C++ type strings (discussed in the next section), your C++ program should include

```
#include <string>
```

For a complete discussion of strings in C, see *C Programming: A Student-Friendly Approach*.

Strings in C++

C++, unlike C, has a `string` type. For example, the following code declares a string variable s and assigns it the C++-type string (an object) converted from the C-type string `"hello"`.

```
        string s;
        s = "hello";    // C++-type string (an object) is assigned to s
```

`string` is not a primitive type. Instead, it is a class. Thus, the s variable declared above is an *object* that contains not only the string itself but a collection of useful functions that operate on the string:

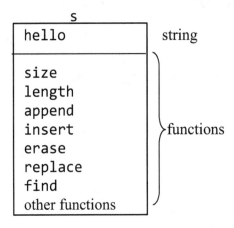

You cannot use the C functions like `strcpy` on C++ type strings. Instead, you should use the member functions in each string object. The program in Fig. 6.1 illustrates the use of some of the functions in a `string` object.

```
 1 // f0601.cpp   Strings
 2 #include <iostream>
 3 #include <string>                    // to use C++ type string functions
 4 using namespace std;
 5 int main()
 6 {
 7     string s = "hello", t;           // initialize s to "hello"
 8     cout << s << endl;               // displays hello
 9     cout << s[1] << endl;            // displays e (char at index 1)
10     cout << s.size() << endl;        // returns number of chars in string
11     cout << s.length() << endl;      // same as size
12     s.append("bye");                 // concats "bye" to end of string
13     cout << s << endl;               // displays hellobye
14     s.insert(5, " ");                // inserts " " (a space) at index 5
15     cout << s << endl;               // displays hello bye
16     s.erase(5, 4);                   // errase 4 chars starting an index 5
17     cout << s << endl;               // displays hello
18     cout << s.find("lo") << endl;    // returns index of substring "lo"
19     s.replace(0, 1, "j");            // replace 1 char at index 0 with "j"
20     cout << s << endl;               // displays jello
21     t = s.substr(1, 2);              // assigns 2-char substr at index 1
22     cout << t << endl;               // displays el
23     cout << s.find("lo") << endl;    // returns indx of substr "lo"
24     if (s == t)                      // compares s and t
25        cout <<  "s and t are equal\n";
26     else
27        cout << "s and t are not equal\n";
28
29     cout << "enter some spaces then hello bye\n";
30     cin >> s; // skips over whitespace, reads in just hello
31     cout << s << endl;          // displays hello
32     cin >> s; // skips over whitespace, reads in bye, no pause
33     cout << s << endl;          // displays bye
34
35     cout << "getline reads leftover newline from preceding cin\n";
36     getline(cin, t);            // reads leftover newline in buffer
37     cout << "outputting t skips next line\n";
38     cout << t << endl;          // displays newline (i.e., moves cursor)
39
40     cout << "enter yes no maybe\n";
41     cin >> t;                   // reads yes
42     cout << t << endl;          // echoes yes
43     cout << "cin.ignore clears buffer so getline works this time\n";
44     cin.ignore(256, '\n');      // clears buffer
45     cout << "enter line" << endl;
46     getline(cin, t);            // reads in entire line, including whitespace
47     cout << t << endl;          // echoes line read in
48     return 0;
49 }
```

Figure 6.1

The file `f0601.out` in the software package shows what the program in Fig. 6.1 will display on your screen if you enter on the keyboard the following strings (include the leading spaces as shown) in response to the prompts:

```
hello bye
yes no maybe
C++ is fun.
```

The best way to study this program is to print out `f0601.out`. Then as you study each line of the program, compare it with the output it produces shown on your printout.

The comments in Fig. 6.1 explain how each function works. Each time `cin` is used for a string input, it skips over whitespace, returning the first sequence of non-whitespace characters it encounters. Thus, line 30 returns only `hello` (not `hello bye`), leaving " bye" and the newline character in the input buffer. The next `cin` (line 32) reads in the leftover non-whitespace still in the buffer (i.e., `bye`). It does not pause for additional keyboard input because it is satisfied by the keyboard entry for line 30.

The `getline` function called on lines 36 and 46 is from the **C++ Standard Library**—it is not a member function in a string object. Thus, it is called without prefixing it with a `string` variable name. `getline` reads an entire line up to and including the newline at the end of the line. It stores the inputted string—except for the newline character—in the `string` variable argument in the call (for example, in the `string` variable t for the call on line 36). However, if there are any leftover characters in the buffer from preceding input—even just the newline character—it reads that instead. Thus, `getline` on line 36 reads the newline leftover from the `cin` on line 32. Because t then contains the newline, line 38 causes the cursor to skip a line. To prevent `getline` from reading what is leftover in the buffer, we use the `cin.ignore` function on line 44 to ignore (i.e., clear) all the characters in the keyboard buffer up to and including the newline character to a maximum of 256 characters, allowing the `getline` on 46 to work properly: It reads the entire line entered in response to the prompt message on line 45.

But how do we copy a string to a string variable? Just use the assignment statement. For example, the following sequence assigns `"yes"` to s, and then assigns s to t. The `cout` displays `yes` twice:

```
string s, t;
s = "yes";        // assign string constant to a string variable
t = s;            // assign a string variable to a string variable
cout << s << " " << t << endl;   // displays yes yes
```

Boolean Variables

C++, unlike C, has a Boolean type `bool` and two `bool` constants: `true` and `false`. For example, the following code declares a `bool` variable b and assigns it `true`:

```
bool b;
b = true;
cout << b << " " << true << " " << false <<endl; // displays 1 1 0
```

Internally, the `bool` constants `true` and `false` are represented by 1 and 0, respectively. In fact, if you output a `bool` variable, you will get 1 or 0. For example, the `cout` above outputs 1 (for b), 1 (for `true`), and 0 (for `false`).

Although C++ has the `bool` type, you can continue to use any non-zero value to represent true, and zero to represent false, just as you did in C.

7 for Loops, Function Templates, and Vectors

for Loops

An array is a data structure that can hold multiple items, one in each of its slots. A `for` loop is generally used to process all the items in an array and other similar data structures. For example, the following code displays all the strings in the `string` array `sa`:

```
string sa[] = {"Amy", "Karen", "Bert"}; // declare and initialize sa
for (int i = 0; i < 3; i++)
   cout << sa[i] << endl;
```

On the first line of a `for` loop, there are three components within the parentheses: the **startup action**, the **exit test**, and the **update action**. The statements *within* each component are *not* terminated with a semicolon. The semicolons simply *separate* the three components. Thus, the update action, `i++`, has no terminating semicolon as it would if it were a standalone statement. Each component can have multiple parts. For example, the following `for` loop is equivalent to the one above, but its update action consists of two parts: the incrementation of `i` and the `cout`. The output of the newline is performed by the `cout` in the update action, not by the `cout` in the body of the loop as in the loop above:

```
for (int i = 0; i < 3; i++, cout << endl)
   cout << sa[i];              two parts in update action separated by a comma
```

We can also process an array using a **range-based `for` loop**, which has a format that is simpler than the standard `for` loop:

```
for (string s: sa)     // range-based for loop
   cout << s << endl;
```

In a range-based `for` loop, within parentheses you declare a variable with the type that matches the type of each slot in the array. Follow that with a colon and the name of the array. Then the `for` loop will execute its body once for each slot of the array. The variable declared within parentheses is assigned the successive slots of the array. For example, in the `for` loop above, `s` is assigned the string in the first slot of the array on the first iteration, the string in the second slot on the second iteration, and so on. Thus, the loop displays all the strings in the `sa` array.

To use a range-based `for` loop on an array, the loop must be in the same scope as the declaration of the array. Otherwise, the compiler will not know the array's size, in which case it would not be able to generate the correct exit test code. Thus, for those situations, you have to use the standard `for` loop and provide the size of the array for use in the exit test. For example, suppose you call a `display` function passing it the `sa` array and its size:

```
display(sa, 3);
```

The `display` function then should be defined as

```
void display(string a[], int size)
{
    for (int i = 0; i < size; i++)
        cout << a[i] << endl;
}
```

Function Templates

When a college creates an acceptance letter for a student who has applied for admission, no one at the college types out the whole letter. Instead, the letter is created from a **template**, which is the acceptance letter missing only the name of the accepted student. Thus, to create the acceptance letter, someone at the college (or perhaps, a computer program) simply fills in the missing name in the template.

The template concept can be applied to functions in C++. A function template is a function in which the type of one or more of its parameters is not specified. When the function is called, the parameters automatically assume the types of the arguments. Thus, the function can work with arguments of any type. For example, the display function in the previous section works only for string arrays. Thus, the call that passes sa works because sa is a string array:

```
display(sa, 3);
```

It, however, would not work for an int array ia:

```
display(ia, 3);   // does not work, argument-parameter mismatch
```

The argument ia in the call is not compatible with the parameter a (whose type is string array) in the function. However, a function template can handle both string and int arrays. Here is the code we need:

```
1 template <typename T>
2 void display(T a[], int size)
3 {
4     for (int i = 0; i < size; i++)
5         cout << a[i] << endl;
6 }
```

Line 1 indicates that T is a placeholder for a type in the function. We then use T on line 2 in place of the type of the a array. When this function is called with

```
display(sa, 3);
```

where sa is a string array, its type (string) in effect replaces T. If this function is called with

```
display(ia, 3);
```

where ia is an int array, its type (int) in effect replaces T. Thus, the function template works for either type. In fact, it works for any type of array whose slots can be outputted by the cout on line 5.

Vectors

The template concept can be extended to a C++ class. In a class template, the underlying type can be represented by a placeholder. When an object is then instantiated from the class, the placeholder is replaced by an actual type.

An example of a class template is vector. The following declaration creates a string vector object v from the vector class, and initializes it with three names:

```
vector<string> sv = {"Ann", "Karen", "Bert"};
```

Note that within angle brackets, the type specified is string. This type then replaces the type placeholder in the vector class. The result is a vector object that holds strings. In we want a vector object that holds int values, we would use

```
vector<int> iv = {10, 20, 30};
```

Vectors and arrays are similar data structures, but they have four significant differences:

1. A vector variable is an object; an array variable is not. Thus, a vector object contains not only a collection of items but also a set of functions that operates on those items.

2. An array cannot grow during runtime. But a vector can, but not really as we shall see. A vector internally is just an array. If an item is to be added to a vector when the vector is already full, the member function that adds an item automatically creates a bigger internal array, copies the current array to the new bigger array, and thereafter uses the bigger array. However, all this is hidden from the user of the vector. Thus, it appears to the user that the vector is actually growing.

3. A vector object contains a data field that holds its current size. Thus, unlike an array, if you pass a vector to a function, you never have to pass its size. Moreover, you can use a range-based for loop to process a vector even if you are out of the scope of the vector's declaration.

4. To use a vector, you must include the header file vector. Arrays (the standard C-type arrays) do not require any header files to be included.

Fig. 7.1 illustrates various features of vectors. Line 8 creates a string vector object v and initializes it with three names. Line 10 displays v using a range-based for loop. Line 12 uses the push_back member function in the v object to push another name onto the "back end" of the v vector. The for loop on line 14 confirms that v now has an additional name. Line 16 uses the pop_back member function to remove the name at the "back end" of the vector v, confirmed by the for loop on 18. Line 20 displays the current size of v using the size member function in the v object. Line 22 displays the name at the front of v (i.e., the first name) using the front member function, the last name using the back member function, the name at index 1 using v[1], and the last name a second time but this time using v[v.size()-1]. Indices start from 0 so v[1] accesses the second name, and vsize() is one more than the index of the last name. Thus, v.size()-1 is the index of the last name. Line 25 uses the empty member function to determine if v is empty. It displays 0 (i.e., false) indicating that v is currently not empty. If v were empty, line 25 would display 1.

```
 1 // f0701.cpp  Vectors
 2 #include <iostream>
 3 #include <string>
 4 #include <vector>
 5 using namespace std;
 6 int main()
 7 {
 8    vector<string> v = {"Ann", "Karen", "Bert"};
 9    cout << "process v with range-based for loop\n";
10    for (string n: v)
11       cout << n << endl;
12    v.push_back("Ernie");
13    cout << "process v after push_back\n";
14    for (string n: v)
15       cout << n << endl;
16    v.pop_back();
17    cout << "process v after pop_back\n";
18    for (string n: v)
19       cout << n << endl;
20    cout << "size of v = " << v.size() << endl;
21    cout << "display of front(), back(), 2nd, last\n";
22    cout << v.front() << " " << v.back() << " " << v[1] << " "
23          << v[v.size()-1] << endl;
24    cout << "display 1/0 if v empty/not empty\n";
25    cout << v.empty() << endl;
26    return 0;
27 }
```

Figure 7.1

Two final notes on vectors: First, the program in Fig. 7.1 illustrates only the member functions in a vector object that you are most likely to need. But there are more. For example, in addition to push_back and pop_back, there are assign (which replaces an element in the vector with a new element at the specified index), insert (which inserts a new element at the specified index, increasing the size of the vector), erase (which removes an element at the specified index), and clear (which removes all the elements in the vector).

Second, an addition to or a removal from a vector using push_back or pop_back affects only one end (the back end). Any list-type data structure used in this way is called a **stack**. In stack terminology, a **push operation** "pushes" (i.e., adds) something onto the "top" (i.e., the back end) of the stack; a **pop operation** "pops" (i.e., removes) something from the "top" (i.e., the back end) of the stack. Because the last item added on a stack is the first item removed, a stack is called a last-in-first-out (LIFO) data structure.

Another common data structure is a queue. A **queue** is a first-in-first-out (FIFO) data structure. Elements are removed from the front of the list and added to the end of the list. Thus, a queue corresponds to the checkout line in a grocery store. New customers enter the line at the end, and the first customer in the line is handled first and therefore is the first out of the line.

8 File Processing

Reading from and Writing to a Text File

cin is called an **input stream**. It is an object associated with the keyboard. To read from cin, we simply use the extraction operator (>>) to read in what is next in the input stream (i.e., the keyboard). To read from a file, we create an input stream object similar to cin but associated with the file we wish to read from. We then use this object just as we use cin. For example, the program in Fig. 8.1 reads from the file t1.txt. Line 8 creates the input stream inFile from the class ifstream, and associates it with the file t1.txt. Line 10 reads in the next "word" in the file into the string variable s (it skips over whitespace and reads in the first block of consecutive non-whitespace characters—thus, it reads one "word"). Each word read into s is displayed on line 11. On end of file or a failure, inFile returns false causing the exit test on line 10 to exit from the loop. The call of the close function in the inFile object on line 12 releases all the computer resources allocated to inFile. Without this line, inFile's resources would still be released when the program ends. Thus, line 12 is unnecessary for this program. However, suppose a program reads from a file only during the first half of its execution. In that case, it makes sense to close the file as soon as it is no longer needed so that the rest of the program can utilize the resources that were allocated to that file.

```
1 // f0801.cpp  Reading from a file
2 #include <iostream>
3 #include <string>
4 #include <fstream> // required for file I/O
5 using namespace std;
6 int main()
7 {
8    ifstream inFile("t1.txt"); // creates inFile associated with t1.txt
9    string s;
10   while (inFile >> s)        // on eof or failure, returns false
11       cout << s << endl;     // display string just read in
12   inFile.close();            // free up resources allocated to inFile
13   return 0;
14 }                        Figure 8.1
```

The file t1.txt contains

```
        t1.txt
┌─────────────┐
│Let us have  │
│fun today.   │
└─────────────┘
```

The program in Fig. 8.1 reads in the words in t1.txt and displays each word on a separate line:

```
Let
us
have
fun
today.
```

Just like cin, inFile skip over whitespace. What is read in each time line 10 is executed depends on the type of s. If s were type char, then each time line 10 is executed, only the next non-whitespace character would be read in. Thus, the output would look like this:

```
L
e
t
u
s
h
:    (continued until the end of the file)
```

Line 8 in Fig. 8.1 is equivalent to the following two statements:

```
ifstream inFile;
inFile.open("t1.txt");
```

The first line creates the inFile input stream. The second line calls the open function in inFile. This function associates the file t1.txt with inFile and allocates to inFile the resources it requires. The close function on line 12 undoes what the open function does.

Line 8 in Fig. 8.1 may fail—for example, if the file t1.txt does not exist. Thus, a check (missing in Fig. 8.1) should be performed to determine if line 8 succeeds or fails. If line 8 fails, inFile returns false (in which case, !inFile would be true). Thus, to determine if line 8 fails, we simply check what inFile returns right after line 8 and take the appropriate action if it indicates a failure:

```
if (!inFile)     // !inFile true if open failed
{
    cout << "The file t1.txt could not be opened.\n";
    exit(1);      // terminate program
}
```

The exit function causes the immediate termination of the program. Its argument is passed back to the operating system. To use exit, include the <cstdlib> header file.

The program in Fig. 8.2 writes to a text file. Recall that a **text file** is a file in which each byte holds a code that represents one character. Examples of text files are t1.txt and any file that holds a C++ source program.

```
 1 // f0802.cpp  Writing to a file
 2 #include <iostream>
 3 #include <string>
 4 #include <fstream>
 5 using namespace std;
 6 int main()
 7 {
 8    ofstream outFile("t2.txt");        // create outFile from ofstream class
 9    outFile << "Have ";                // output "Have "
10    outFile << "fun." << endl;         // output "fun." followed by newline
11    outFile.close();
12    return 0;
13 }                                Figure 8.2
```

Line 8 in Fig. 8.2 creates the outFile output stream from the class ofstream and associates it with the file to be created (t2.txt). If t2.txt already exists, it will be replaced by the output produced by the program. Line 9 outputs a string to t2.txt. Line 10 then outputs a second string followed by the newline character (from endl). Line 11 then closes the file, which releases any of the computer resources allocated to the outFile output stream. But, more important, it flushes any output that remains in the output buffer which has not yet been written to the t2.txt file. When lines 9 and 10 are executed, the strings they output are not necessarily immediately written to t2.txt. Typically, they are stored in a **buffer** (a temporary storage area in computer memory). When the buffer becomes full from repeated outputs, only then are its contents written to the output file. Thus, right after lines 9 and 10 are executed, t2.txt may still be empty. But the close function on line 11 forces any remaining output in the buffer to be flushed (i.e., written to the output file). If line 11 were not present, nothing may be written to t2.txt. *Rule*: Always close output files. Here is what is in the t2.txt file created by the program:

```
        t2.txt
      ┌──────────┐
      │Have fun. │
      └──────────┘
```

The output produced by the program in Fig. 8.2 *replaces* whatever is in t2.txt if t2.txt already exists. Thus, if you repeatedly execute the program, the resulting t2.txt file will always be the same. The program in Fig. 8.3 also writes to t2.txt, but it *appends* what it outputs to the back end of what is already in t2.txt. Thus, each time you execute it, it will append "Don't worry." to t2.txt. If you execute it 10 times, then there will be 10 lines added to t2.txt, each with "Don't worry.".

The difference between the programs in Fig. 8.2 and 8.3 is on line 8 in Fig. 8.3. In addition to the file name, we specified a **file mode**: ios::app, which indicates output to the file should be *appended* to the end of the file if it already exists. If the program in Fig. 8.3 is executed once after the program in Fig. 8.2 is executed, t2.txt will look like this:

```
        t2.txt
      ┌────────────┐
      │Have fun.   │
      │Don't worry.│
      └────────────┘
```

```
 1 // f0803.cpp  Appending to a file
 2 #include <iostream>
 3 #include <string>
 4 #include <fstream>
 5 using namespace std;
 6 int main()
 7 {
 8     ofstream outFile("t2.txt", ios::app); // os::app means append
 9     outFile << "Don't ";
10     outFile << "worry." << endl;
11     outFile.close();
12     return 0;
13 }
```

Figure 8.3

The program in Fig. 8.1 reads one word at a time. More precisely, it skips over whitespace and reads the first block of consecutive non-whitespace it encounters. The program in Fig. 8.4 reads one entire line at a time. The arguments in the call of getline on line 12 are the input stream inFile and the string variable s. Each time line 12 is executed, it reads in the entire next line (including whitespace) in the file t1.txt. Line 15 then displays the line just read in. On end of file, the input stream object, inFile, returns false which causes line 14 to break out of the loop.

```
 1 // f0804.cpp  Using getline
 2 #include <iostream>
 3 #include <string>
 4 #include <fstream>
 5 using namespace std;
 6 int main()
 7 {
 8    ifstream inFile("t1.txt");
 9    string s;
10    while (true)
11    {
12       getline(inFile, s);        // read one line from text file
13       if (!inFile)               // inFile returns false on end of file
14          break;                  // exit loop
15       cout << s << endl;         // display line just read in
16    }
17    return 0;
18 }
```

Figure 8.4

Reading from and Writing to a Binary File

Fig. 8.5 shows how to read a binary file. A **binary file** is any file that is not a text file. Thus, each byte in a binary file does *not* contain the code for a character. Example of binary files are b1.bin created by the program in Fig. 8.5 and any file that holds the executable form of a C++ program.

Some computer systems perform a translation when it is reads from or writes to a file. For example, Windows translates the return/newline sequence to just the newline character. It does the reverse on an output operation. When reading from or writing to a binary file, this translation should be prevented. Otherwise, on input the program would not get the exact contents of the file it is reading if the file coincidentally contains the return/newline sequence (it would get just the newline character). On output, the output file would not get exactly what the program is outputting if it outputs the newline character (it would get the return/newline sequence). To prevent this translation, lines 8 and 13 in Fig. 8.5 specify the file mode ios::binary.

```
1  // f0805.cpp  Reading and writing a binary file
2  #include <iostream>
3  #include <string>
4  #include <fstream>
5  using namespace std;
6  int main()
7  {
8     ofstream outFile("b1.bin", ios::binary);   // stops translation
9     for (int i = 1; i < 3; i++)
10       outFile.write((char *)&i, sizeof(int)); // outputs 1 and 2
11    outFile.close();
12
13    ifstream inFile("b1.bin", ios::binary);    // stops translation
14    int i;
15    while (true)
16    {
17       inFile.read((char *)&i, sizeof(int));
18       if (!inFile)       // inFile goes false on end of file
19          break;
20       cout << i << endl; // displays 1 and 2 on separate lines
21    }
22    return 0;
23 }
```

Figure 8.5

Line 10 uses the write function in the outFile object to output the contents of the int variable i in its raw binary form to b1.bin. The first argument in the call of write should be the address of the location in memory to be outputted. This address must have the type char *. Thus, we cast &i (which has the type int *) to char *. The second argument is the number of bytes to output.

The first time line 10 is executed, i contains 1. Thus, it outputs the 32-bit binary number 0...01. If your computer is a **little endian** system, it outputs the bytes in the number from the "little end" to the "big end" (i.e., from right to left). Thus, the file receives the bytes in this order: 00000001 00000000

00000000 00000000. To confirm this, after running the program in Fig. 8.5, compile the program `look.c` in the software package by entering

```
g++ look.c -o look
```

Then enter

```
look b1.bin
```
(or `./look b1.bin` on a non-Windows system)

The `look` program will then display `b1.bin` in binary, decimal, and hex:

```
Program = look      Input file = b1.bin        Mon Mar 25 09:10:49 2024

Bytes starting at address 0 decimal = 0 hex:
00000001 00000000 00000000 00000000 00000010 00000000 00000000 00000000

Characters:


Decimal:
   1        0         0         0         2         0         0         0

Hex:
  01        00        00        00        02        00        00        00
-------------------------------------------------------------------------
```

It does not display any characters because none of the bytes in the file contain a code for a displayable character. The display confirms that the computer on which `b1.bin` was created is little endian. For the number 1, its low order (i.e., its rightmost bye) appears first. When reading the binary output from a little endian computer, you should mentally reverse the bytes for each number. For example, you should read the first four bytes as 00000000 00000000 00000000 00000001.

Getting back to the program in Fig. 8.5, the second half reads and displays the numbers in `b1.bin`. To read each number, we use the `read` function in the `inFile` object on line 17. The types of its two parameters are the same as for the `write` function (a `char *` address and the number of bytes). When a number is read from the file, no conversion takes place. The binary number in `b1.bin` is simply read in, as is, into the variable `i`. In contrast, when an integer in a text file is read into an `int` variable, it must be converted from its character form to the corresponding raw binary form. Line 20 displays the binary number now in the variable `i`. Note that line 20 does perform a conversion: from the raw binary form to the decimal form displayable on the screen.

9 Overloading Operators

Overloading +

The plus sign (+) is an overloaded operator. That is, the context in which it appears determines what it does. Specifically, if its operands are numbers, it adds, but if its operands are strings, it concatenates. But the plus sign does not work if its operands are objects instantiated from classes you write. However, we can further overload the plus sign so it works for any type of object as well as for numbers and strings.

In the expression x + y, the operator + is between its two operands, x and y. We call this notation **infix notation**. The same expression in **prefix notation** (operator first, then the operands) is +(x, y) from which you can see that an arithmetic expression is really a function call. The plus sign is the name of the function, and the operands are the arguments passed to the function. To overload the plus sign for some type of object, we define the + function that performs the operation we want the plus sign to perform for that type. The program in Fig. 9.1 overloads the plus sign so it works for Number objects.

```cpp
1 // f0901.cpp  Overloading +
2 #include <iostream>
3 using namespace std;
4 class Number
5 {
6    public:
7       void display();
8       Number operator +(Number);
9    private:
10      int x = 1;
11 };
12 void Number::display()
13 {
14    cout << x << endl;
15 }
16 Number Number::operator +(Number right)
17 {
18    Number n;
19    n.x = x + right.x;  // n.x is in n, x is in n1, right.x is in n2
20    return n;
21 }
22 //====================================
23 int main()
24 {
25    Number n1, n2, n3;
26    n3 = n1 + n2;           // using overloaded +
27    n3.display();           // displays 2
28    return 0;
29 }
```

Figure 9.1

Line 25 in Fig. 9.1 creates three objects, n1, n2, and n3 of type Number. Line 26 then adds n1 and n2, and assigns the result (in a new Number object) to n3.

The + function that defines what the plus sign does for Number operands is on lines 16 to 21. *Every* Number object has this function. When line 26

```
26    n3 = n1 + n2;
```

is executed, the + function in the *left* operand (i.e., in n1) is automatically called, passing it the right operand (i.e., n2) as an argument. Thus, on line 19,

```
19    n.x = x + right.x;   // n.x is in n, x is in n1, right.x is in n2
```

the first x on the right side of the assignment statement is the x in n1. right is the parameter that is passed n2 so right.x is the x in n2. n is a local variable of type Number. Thus, line 19 sums the x in n1 with the x in n2 and assigns the result to the x in n. Finally, line 20

```
20    return n;
```

returns a copy of n back to line 26. Line 26 then assigns it to n3. The x variable in n1 and n2 contains 1. Thus, the + function creates a Number object whose x value contains 2. A copy of this object is then assigned to n3.

The + function is set up like any other function in a class. Its prototype appears in the class (see line 8). Its only unique features are its name (an operator) and the reserved word operator on lines 8 and 16 that tells the compiler that the plus sign is an overloaded operator—not an ordinary plus sign.

Overloading ==

In the previous example, the overloaded operator returns an object that has the same type as its operands. The program in Fig. 9.2 does something different: It overloads the equality operator, ==, so that it compares two Number objects. It does not return an object. Instead, it returns a bool value—true or false—based on the comparison of the two objects.

```
1 // f0902.cpp  Overloading ==
2 #include <iostream>
3 using namespace std;
4 class Number
5 {
6    public:
7        void set(int);
8        bool operator ==(Number);
9    private:
10        int x = 1;
11 };
```

```
12 void Number::set(int i)
13 {
14    x = i;
15 }
16 bool Number::operator ==(Number right)
17 {
18    if (x == right.x)  // x in n1, right.x in n2
19       return true;
20    else
21       return false;
22 }
23 //=====================================
24 int main()
25 {
26    Number n1, n2;
27    cout << (n1 == n2) << endl;  // returns 1 (i.e., true)
28    n1.set(2);
29    cout << (n1 == n2) << endl;  // returns 0 (i.e., false)
30    return 0;
31 }
```

Figure 9.2

Line 27 compares the n1 and n2 objects. They are identical so true (represented by 1) is returned. Line 28 then modifies the n1 object so n1 and n2 are no longer identical. Thus, the comparsion on line 29 returns false (represented by 0).

Both n1 and n2 have a set and a == function. When the comparison on line 27 is performed, the == function in the *left* operand (n1) is called. This call passes the right operand (n2) to the == function. Thus, on line 18,

```
18    if (x == right.x)  // x is in n1, right.x is in n2
```

the x on the left is the x in n1. The parameter right receives n2. Thus, right.x is the x in n2. Line 18 compares the two x's and returns true or false accordingly.

If the Number class had multiple instance variables, the == function would have to do multiple comparisons to determine if all the variables in the left operand equaled the corresponding variables in the right operand. In that case, if all the corresponding variables were equal, the == function would return true. Otherwise, it would return false.

Overloading Unary –

Before we learn how to overload the unary minus size so that is works for a Number object, let's review how the ordinary unary minus sign works in C++. Our overloaded version should work the same way. Consider the following code:

```
int x = 1, y;
y = -x;
cout << "x = " << x << " y = " << endl;      // displays x = 1 y = -1
```

The assignment to y assigns the negation of the value in x. It does *not* modify the value in x. Thus, the cout statement displays

```
x = 1 y = -1
```

Our overloaded unary minus should work in exactly the same way. For example, consider the main function in Fig. 9.3:

```
23 int main()
24 {
25     Number n, m;
26     n.display();  // displays 1
27     m = -n;       // does not affect n
28     n.display();  // x in n is still 1
29     m.display();  // x in m is -1 (the negation of x in n)
30     n = -n;       // negates n itself
31     n.display();  // x in n now -1
32     return 0;
33 }
```

The n and m Number objects have an instance variable x whose initial value is 1. Line 26 displays the x in n, which is 1:

```
1
```

Line 27 then assigns to m the negation of a *copy* of n. It does not modify the n object. Thus, x in n is still 1 and the x in m is -1. Line 28 displays x in n. It is still 1:

```
1
```

Line 29 displays the x in m. It contains the negation of x in n:

```
-1
```

Line 30 assigns the negation of n *back to* n. Thus, this statement negates the x in n itself. Line 31 displays the modified x in n:

```
-1
```

One question you may still have is how does the unary minus function in the n object get a copy of the n object so it can negate and return it. Recall that whenever a member function in an object is called, it is *always* passed the pointer to the object. This pointer is received by the special parameter this. Thus, to get a copy of the object, the unary minus function simply dereferences this:

```
18    Number z = *this;    // initialize z with a copy of the n object
```

Line 18 initializes z using the object (obtained by dereferencing this). Line 19 negates the x in z. Line 20 then returns z, which is then assigned to m on line 27.

```cpp
1 // f0903.cpp  Overloading unary -
2 #include <iostream>
3 using namespace std;
4 class Number
5 {
6    public:
7        void display();
8        Number operator -();
9    private:
10       int x = 1;
11 };
12 void Number::display()
13 {
14    cout << x << endl;
15 }
16 Number Number::operator -()
17 {
18    Number z = *this;     // initialize z with a copy of the n object
19    z.x = -x;             // negate x in n, assign to x in z
20    return z;             // return z
21 }
22 //======================================
23 int main()
24 {
25    Number n, m;
26    n.display();  // displays 1
27    m = -n;       // does not affect n, invokes operator function in n
28    n.display();  // x in n is still 1
29    m.display();  // x in m is -1 (the negation of x in n)
30    n = -n;       // negates n itself
31    n.display();  // x in n now -1
32    return 0;
33 }
```
Figure 9.3

Overloading + when the Operands Have Different Types

In the program in Fig. 9.1, both operands of the overloaded + operator have the same type (i.e., Number). In the program in Fig. 9.4, the left operand of the overloaded + operator has the type Number, but the right operand has the type int:

```cpp
26    n3 = n1 + 7;
```

```
 1 // f0904.cpp  Overloading Number + int
 2 #include <iostream>
 3 using namespace std;
 4 class Number
 5 {
 6    public:
 7        void display();
 8        Number operator +(int);
 9    private:
10        int x = 1;
11 };
12 void Number::display()
13 {
14    cout << x << endl;
15 }
16 Number Number::operator +(int i)
17 {
18    Number n;
19    n.x = x + i;     // n.x in n, x in n1
20    return n;
21 }
22 //=====================================
23 int main()
24 {
25    Number n1, n3;
26    n3 = n1 + 7;
27    n3.display();          // displays 8
28    return 0;
29 }
```

Figure 9.4

When line 26 is executed, the 1 in the x in n1 and 7 are added. The result 8 is stored in the x in the local variable n. Line 20 returns n. Line 26 then assigns the returned object to n3. Thus, line 27, which displays the x in n3, displays 8. The program in Fig. 9.4 is the program in Fig. 9.1 with minimal modifications: Lines 8 and 16 specify int in place of Number, and line 26 adds 7 to n1 instead of adding n2 to n1.

When an expression that uses an overloaded binary operator is evaluated, the operator function in the *left operand* is automatically executed. For this reason, the *left operand* must be an object that contains the operator function. In Fig. 9.4, the + function is in Number objects. Thus, the left operand has to be a Number object. It *cannot* be an *int*. Thus, this approach to overloading operators can handle a statement like

```
n3 = n1 + 7;
```

But it cannot handle a statement like

```
n3 = 7 + n1;
```

We will see a solution to this shortcoming in the next section.

Overloading Operators with Friend Functions

A **friend function** is a function that is *not* a member of a class. To make it a "friend"—not a member—of a class, its prototype must appear inside the definition of that class prefixed by the reserved word `friend` (see lines 8, 9, and 10 in Fig. 9.5).

What makes a friend function special is that is that it can directly access the private members of the class to which it is friend. However, unlike a member function in a class, a friend function it not automatically passed the address of an object when it is called. Thus, to provide a friend function access to an object, it must be passed that object as an argument in the function call.

```cpp
1  // f0905.cpp  Overloading + with friends
2  #include <iostream>
3  using namespace std;
4  class Number
5  {
6     public:
7        void display();
8        friend Number operator +(Number, Number);
9        friend Number operator +(Number, int);
10       friend Number operator +(int, Number);
11    private:
12       int x = 1;
13 };
14 void Number::display()
15 {
16    cout << x << endl;
17 }
18 //====================================
19 Number operator +(Number left, Number right)
20 {
21    Number n;
22    n.x = left.x + right.x;
23    return n;
24 }
25 Number operator +(Number left, int right)
26 {
27    Number n;
28    n.x = left.x + right;
29    return n;
30 }
31 Number operator +(int left, Number right)
32 {
33    Number n;
34    n.x = left + right.x;
35    return n;
36 }
37 //====================================
```

```
38 int main()
39 {
40     Number n1, n3;
41     n3 = n1 + n3;
42     n3.display();          // displays 2
43     n3 = n1 + 7;
44     n3.display();          // displays 8
45     n3 = 10 + n1;
46     n3.display();          // displays 11
47     return 0;
48 }
```

Figure 9.5

Let's see how we can put friend functions to good use in operator overloading. In Fig. 9.5, we overload the + operator. There are three + functions. All three are regular functions. That is, they are *not* a member function of some class. The first + function handles expressions in which both operands have the type Number (see line 8). The second handles expressions in which the left operand has the type Number and the right operand has the type int (see line 9). The third handles expressions in which the left operand has the type int and the right operand has the type Number (see line 10).

Because the three + functions are friends of the Number class, they can access the private x variable in a Number object. When line 41 is executed,

```
41     n3 = n1 + n3;
```

the + function compatible with the operands n1 and n2 is automatically called (i.e., the + function on lines 19 to 24 with two Number parameters is called). This call passes both n1 and n2 to this + function. In similar fashion, when line 43 is executed,

```
43     n3 = n1 + 7;
```

n1 and 7 are passed to the compatible + function on lines 25 to 30. When line 45 is executed,

```
45     n3 = 10 + n1;
```

10 and n1 are passed to the compatible + function on lines 31 to 36. All three + functions compute a sum and store it the x variable in the local variable n. The object n then is then returned to main where it is assigned to n3.

The "standard" approach for overloading an operator puts the operator function in the class as a member as we did in Figures 9.1, 9.2, 9.3, and 9.4. This makes sense because it puts everything about the class inside the class, making a nice complete package. But this method does not always work depending of the type of the left operand of the overloaded operator. For example, the standard approach used in Fig. 9.4 cannot handle the case where the left operand is an int. For those cases, we have to use friend functions, as we did in Fig. 9.5. The result is not as "clean" as the standard approach because the operator functions are outside the class. But it gets the job done.

10 Inheritance and Virtual Functions

Inheritance

This chapter is complicated. But as Mr. Spock would say on Star Trek, it's logical. So it all makes sense. Just take your time reading it.

Inheritance in C++ is a mechanism that defines a new class from a class that already exists. We call the new class the **derived class** (or the **subclass**) and the original class the **base class** (or the **superclass**). The derived class "inherits" (i.e., automatically includes) all the members in the base class. Inheritance establishes a class hierarchy: The derived class is one level lower in the hierarchy than the base class from which it is derived.

In the program in Fig. 10.1, A is the base class and B is the derived class. Thus, an object created from the B class inherits all the members of the A class. That is, it contains all the members in the B class plus all the members inherited from the A class. We call an object created from the A class an A-*level object* and an object created from the B class a B-*level object*.

Line 43 in Fig. 10.1 creates an A-level object with

```
43    aptr = new A();
```

Line 46 creates a B-level object with

```
46    bptr = new B();
```

The A class contains a `set` function, a `display` function, and an x field. Thus, the A-level object contains these three members. The B class contains a `set` function, a `display` function, and a y field. Thus, the B-level object contains these members. But it also contains the members of the A class through inheritance. Thus, it contains two `set` functions, two `display` functions, an x variable, and a y variable. Conceptually, here are the contents of these objects and the pointers that point to them:

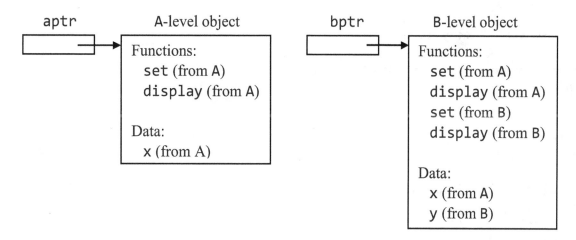

The "`public A`" following "`class B`" on line 21 in Fig. 10.1 indicates that B is derived from A:

```
21 class B: public A        // indicates B is derived from A
```

```
1 // f1001.cpp   Inheritance
2 #include <iostream>
3 using namespace std;
4 class A
5 {
6    public:
7        void set(int n);
8        void display();
9    protected:         // allows access from derived classes
10       int x;
11 };
12 void A::set(int n)
13 {
14    x = n;
15 }
16 void A::display()
17 {
18    cout << x << endl;
19 }
20 //===================
21 class B: public A
22 {
23    public:
24        void set(int n, int m);
25        void display();
26    private:
27        int y;
28 };
29 void B::set(int n, int m)
30 {
31    x = n;
32    y = m;
33 }
34 void B::display()
35 {
36    cout << x << " " << y << endl;
37 }
38 //===============================
39 int main()
40 {
41    A *aptr;
42    B *bptr;
43    aptr = new A();
44    aptr->set(1);
45    aptr->display();  // displays 1
46    bptr = new B();
47    bptr->set(2, 3);  // displays 2 3
48    bptr->display();
49    aptr = bptr;
50    aptr->display();  // displays 2
51    return 0;
52 }
```

Indicates B is derived from A

Figure 10.1

The keyword `public` on this line indicates that the members in the B class that are inherited from the A class have the same accessibility in the B class as they do in the A class. For example, because the `set` function in the A class is public, then it is also public in the B class. If, however, we replace the keyword `public` on line 21 with `private`, then all the members inherited from the A class are private in the B class.

The `protected` keyword on line 9 restricts the accessibility of x to A and the classes derived from A. For example, if B is derived from A, and C is derived from B, then x is accessible from A, B, and C. Thus, a class member that is protected is more accessible than a private member but less accessible than a public member.

The C++ program has two `set` functions (one from class A and one from class B) and two `display` functions (one from class A and one from class B). Which of the two `set` functions is called depends on the level of the pointer in the calling statement. Similarly, which of the two `display` functions is called depends on the level of the pointer in the calling statement. For example, in line 45, the pointer (`aptr`) is an A-level pointer (i.e., it is declared as a pointer to an A-level object). Thus, the compiler translates the call of the `display` function to a call of the `display` function from the A class. On line 48, the pointer (`bptr`) is a B-level pointer. Thus, the compiler translates this call of the `display` function to a call of the `display` function from the B class.

In the C++ program in Fig. 10.1, the two `display` functions have the same name as well as the two `set` functions. But in the assembler version, their mangled names are distinct. Each starts with the class name bracketed with at-signs. For example, the names for the A-level `display` function and the B-level `display` function are `@A@display$v` and `@B@display$v`, respectively. The class name at the beginning of their mangled names distinguishes the two names.

A B-level object *contains all the members from the A class* plus the members of the B class. Thus, you can think of a B-level object as an A object with some extra stuff in it, the extra stuff being the members defined in the B class. The pointer `aptr` is an A-level pointer. Thus, it is *required* to point to an A object. But because a B-level object is an A object with some extra stuff, it is perfectly legal for `aptr` to point to a B-level object. Thus, the statement on line 49 in Fig. 10.1 is legal:

```
49      aptr = bptr;
```

We get the following structure.

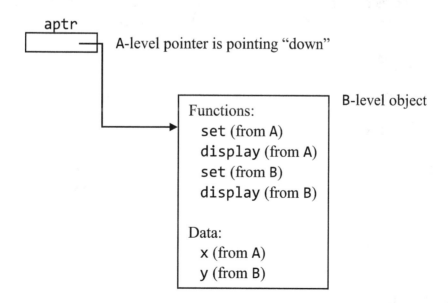

Recall that the base class is higher in the class hierarchy than the derived class. Thus, in the preceding program, A-level pointers and objects are higher than B-level pointers and objects. Because in the structure illustrated above, `aptr` (an A-level pointer) is pointing to an object lower in the class hierarchy (a B-level object), we say `aptr` is pointing "down." But now suppose we replace line 49 in the C++ with

```
bptr = aptr;
```

We are attempting to get the following structure:

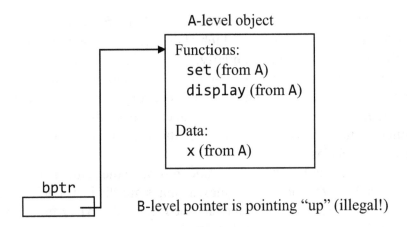

B-level pointer is pointing "up" (illegal!)

This statement is attempting to assign to a B-level pointer (`bptr`) a pointer to an A-level object (the pointer in `aptr`). A B-level pointer is required to point to an object that has all the members in the B class. But an A-level object does not have any of the members in the B class. Thus, `bptr` cannot be assigned a pointer to an A-level object.

Because of inheritance, if an object pointer is pointing down in the class hierarchy, the object to which it points necessarily has all the class members of the class at the pointer's level. Thus, an object pointer pointing down is legal. However, if an object pointer is pointing up, the object to which it points does not have any of the class members of the class at the pointer's level. Thus, an object pointer pointing up is not legal. Here is a simple statement on the restrictions on object pointers:

Rule: An object pointer can point "across" (i.e., to an object at its own level) or "down" (i.e., to an object at a lower level derived from its level) but not up (i.e., to object at a higher level).

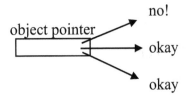

Incidentally, at line 50, `aptr` is pointing down to a B-level object which therefore has both x and y variables. But because `aptr` is an A-level pointer, the compiler translates the line to a call of the `display` function from the A class. Thus, only the x variable of the object is displayed.

Rule: The function called in an object depends on the level of the pointer pointing to the object—not on the level of the object pointed to.

As we will see in the next section, this rule does not apply if the function is a virtual function.

Virtual Functions

The following program is identical to the C++ program in the preceding section except for a small modification on line 8: The keyword `virtual` makes the `display` function a virtual function. It also causes any `display` function with the same signature (i.e., with same name and the same parameter list encoding) in any derived class to be virtual as well. Thus, the `display` function in the B class on line 25 is also virtual.

```cpp
1 // f1002.cpp  Virtual functions
2 #include <iostream>
3 using namespace std;
4 class A
5 {
6    public:
7        void set(int n);
8        virtual void display();  // display now a virtual function
9    protected:
10        int x;
11 };
12 void A::set(int n)
13 {
14    x = n;
15 }
16 void A::display()
17 {
18    cout << x << endl;
19 }
20 //===================
21 class B: public A
22 {
23    public:
24        void set(int n, int m);
25        void display();           // this display also virtual
26    private:
27        int y;
28 };
29 void B::set(int n, int m)
30 {
31    x = n;
32    y = m;
33 }
34 void B::display()
35 {
36    cout << x << " " << y << endl;
37 }
38 //==============================
```

```
39 int main()
40 {
41    A *aptr;
42    B *bptr;
43    aptr = new A();    // aptr pointing across to A-level object
44    aptr->set(1);
45    aptr->display();   // A-level display called
46    bptr = new B();    // bptr pointing across to B-level object
47    bptr->set(2, 3);
48    bptr->display();   // B-level display called
49    aptr = bptr;       // aptr now pointing down to B-level object
50    aptr->display();   // B-level display called
51    return 0;
52 }
```

Figure 10.2

If a pointer is pointing to an object with a virtual function, it is the object—not the pointer—that determines the function called. For example, on line 50, the display function is called. aptr (an A-level pointer) at this point is pointing to a B-level object which has both the inherited A-level display function and the B-level display function. Because display is a virtual function, it is the level of the object that determines which display function is called. Because the object is a B-level object, the B-level display function is called, which displays the x and y variables in the B-level object. If the display function is not virtual, as it was in Fig. 10.1, then the level of the pointer determines which display function is called. In that case, because the aptr is an A-level pointer, the A-level display function would be called which would display only the x variable in the B object.

Output with the virtual keyword:

```
1
2 3
2 3            (B-level display function called)
```

Output without the virtual keyword:

```
1
2 3
2              (A-level display function called)
```

An important question to consider at this point is how the compiler *at compile* time can determine on line 50 in Fig. 10.2 what type of object (A-level or B-level) aptr will point to *at runtime*. You might argue that the compiler knows what is in aptr from the assignment statement on line 49, which assigns bptr to aptr. bptr is a B-level pointer. Thus, bptr must be pointing to a B-level object, and therefore so must aptr after the assignment on line 49. Unfortunately, a compiler cannot always determine at compile time what will be in an object pointer at runtime. Here is a code segment in which such is the case (suppose it replaces lines 49 and 50 in Fig. 10.2):

```
51 cin > z;
52 if (z < 0)
53    aptr = new A();          // creates A-level object. Pointer assigned to aptr.
54 else
55    aptr = new B();          // creates B-level object. Pointer assigned to aptr.
56 aptr->display();            // impossible to know at compile time what is in aptr.
```

If the value entered for z is negative, then aptr is assigned a pointer to an A-level object. But if the value entered is non-negative, aptr is assigned a pointer to a B-level object, in which case aptr is pointing down. Thus, what aptr points to at runtime depends on what the user enters for z *at runtime*. Clearly, the compiler has no way of knowing at *compile time* what the user will enter for z at runtime. Furthermore, the situation can be even more complicated. Suppose the code above is in a loop. Then translating the call of the display function to *either* the A-level display function or the B-level display function is incorrect. If, for example, the compiler translates the call to a call of the A-level display function, then the call is incorrect on any iteration of the loop in which a non-negative value is entered for z. If, on the other hand, the compiler translates the call to the B-level display function, then the call is incorrect on any iteration of the loop in which a negative value is entered for z. Thus, it appears that there is *no correct way for the compiler to translate the call of* display on line 56. But if you compile the code above with any standard C++ compiler and run it, it works the way it is supposed to: That is, if the object is an A-level object, then the A-level display function is called; if the object is a B-level object, then the B-level function is called. So how is this seemingly impossible task accomplished? The answer is really very simple: The compiler generates code that *at runtime* determines the appropriate display function to call.

To understand how calls of virtual functions are translated to assembly language, let's first examine the underlying data structures that exist as a result of lines 43 and 46 in Fig. 10.2, first if the display function is not a virtual function and then if the display function is a virtual function.

If the display function is *not* virtual, then this is what aptr points to:

If the display function is not virtual, then this is what bptr points to:

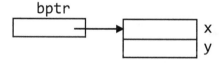

Now let's consider the case in which the display function is declared virtual. We get different structures.

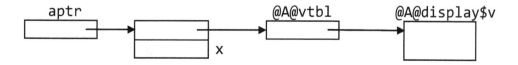

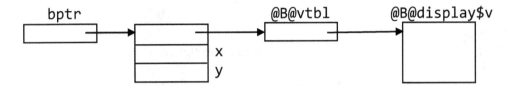

Now both objects start with an extra field: a pointer to a *virtual function table*, which in turn points to the virtual functions for that object. A B-level object contains two virtual functions: the `display` function inherited from the A class and the B-level `display` function. But the virtual function table for a B object points to only the B-level `display` function. Thus, if `bptr` is assigned to `aptr`, then `aptr` will point to the structure whose virtual table points to the B-level `display` function. Thus, `aptr->display()` executes the B-level `display` function.

Constructors and Inheritance

As you already know, objects are typically initialized when they are created with a special function called a constructor. Let's first review constructors and then see how they work in a program that uses inheritance.

The name of a constructor must be identical to the name of the class and it has no return type. For example, the program in Fig. 10.3 has a class A in which a constructor is declared (line 7). Note that its name is identical to the class name.

A constructor is defined in the same way other member functions are defined. For example, the first line of the definition of the `display` function in the A class on line 16 in Fig. 10.2 starts with

```
16 void A::display()
```

It consists of the return type (`void`), the class name (`A`), the double colon, the function name (`display`), and the parameter list within parentheses. The definition of the constructor in the A class in Fig.. 10.3 has the same components, except it has no return type:

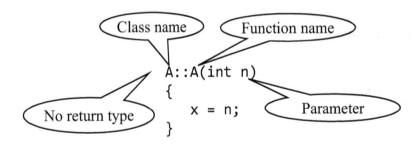

If we declare an object of type A with

```
42     A a(1);                  // x initialized with 1
```

the A constructor is automatically called and passed the argument 1. The constructor, as defined, then initializes x in the object with 1. The constructor is also called if we allocate the object dynamically using the new operator:

```
46     aptr = new A(4);         // x initialized with 4
```

We have the same situation with the B class with one complication. Because the B class is derived from the A class, the B class inherits the x field from the A class. Thus, the B constructor should initialize x as well as y. The best way to do this is to have the B constructor call the A constructor passing it the initial value of x. We specify this on the first line of the definition for the constructor for B by appending a colon to it followed by a call of the A constructor:

```
29 B::B(int n, int m): A(n)
```

calls A constructor passing it n

```
 1 // f1003.cpp  Constructors
 2 #include <iostream>
 3 using namespace std;
 4 class A
 5 {
 6    public:
 7        A(int n);
 8        void display();
 9    protected:
10        int x;
11 };
12 A::A(int n)
13 {
14    x = n;
15 }
16 void A::display()
17 {
18    cout << x << endl;
19 }
20 //===================
21 class B: public A
22 {
23    public:
24        B(int n, int m);
25        void display();
26    private:
27        int y;
28 };
29 B::B(int n, int m): A(n)
30 {
31    y = m;
32 }
33 void B::display()
34 {
35    cout << x << " " << y << endl;
36 }
37 //=============================
```

Constructor prototype

Constructor definition

Constructor prototype

Constructor definition

```
38 int main()
39 {
40    A *aptr;
41    B *bptr;
42    A a(1);
43    a.display();          // displays 1
44    B b(2, 3);
45    b.display();          // displays 2 3
46    aptr = new A(4);
47    aptr->display();      // displays 4
48    bptr = new B(5, 6);
49    bptr->display();      // displays 5 6
50    return 0;
51 }
```

Figure 10.3

The output produced by the C++ program in Fig. 10.3 is

```
1
2 3
4
5 6
```

Constructors can be overloaded. For example, we can have three constructors in B, each with a different parameter list:

```
B::B(): A(1)
{
    y = 2;          // inherited x initialized to 1
}
B::B(int n): A(1)
{
    y = n;          // inherited x initialized to 1
}
B::B(int n, int m): A(n)
{
    y = m;          // inherited x initialized to n
}
```

Then the constructor called depends on the argument list in the call. For example, the declaration

```
B b1();          // calls first constructor
```

calls the first constructor above because its argument list matches the parameter list in that constructor. Similarly, following declarations call the second and third constructors, respectively:

```
B b2(2);          // calls second constructor
B b3(2, 3);       // calls third constructor
```

11 Exceptions

try and catch Blocks

An **exception** is an unusual condition or error that occurs during the execution of a program. In most cases, exceptions are errors. When an exception occurs, the program "throws" the exception. That is, it creates an object that represents the exception. If the "thrown" exception is not "caught" (i.e., intercepted and processed), it forces the termination of the program.

    The easiest way to understand how exceptions work is to study several simple programs in which exceptions occur. In our first example (Fig. 11.1), line 7 throws an exception.

```
 1 // f1101.cpp  Exceptions
 2 #include <iostream>
 3 using namespace std;
 4 int main()
 5 {
 6    string s = "a";
 7    s.erase(2);               // invalid index, throws an exception
 8    cout << "after error\n"; // not executed
 9    return 0;
10 }
```

Figure 11.1

Because the size of the s string is 1, any index larger than 1 is invalid. Thus, the argument 2 in the call of erase on line 7 is an invalid index. The erase function responds by throwing an exception which causes the immediate termination of the program. Thus, line 8 is never executed. The somewhat cryptic error message displayed on the screen is

```
terminate called after throwing an instance of 'std::out_of_range'
  what():  basic_string::erase: __pos (which is 2) > this->size() (which is 1)
```

It indicates that the type of the exception is out_of_range (see the end of the first line). what is a function in exception objects that displays information on the exception. This one indicates that the argument (which is 2) in the call of erase is greater than the size (which is 1) of the string.

    Our next example uses a try and a catch block. If an exception is thrown within the try block, the catch block that follows it "catches" (i.e., intercepts) the exception. After the catch block completes, normal execution resumes with the statement that follows the catch block unless a statement within the catch block terminates execution (such as a call of the exit function). The exception thrown by line 9 in Fig. 11.2 is automatically passed to the e parameter on line 11. The ampersand ("&") on line 11 makes e a reference parameter. We use pass by reference because it is more efficient than pass by value.

```
 1 // f1102.cpp  try/catch blocks
 2 #include <iostream>
 3 using namespace std;
 4 int main()
 5 {
 6    string s = "a";
 7    try
 8    {
 9       s.erase(2);                    // throws out_of_range exception
10    }
11    catch (exception &e)          // catches exception
12    {
13       cout << "in catch block\n";
14       cout << e.what() << endl;    // displays error message
15    }
16    cout << "after catch block\n";  // executed after catch block
17    return 0;
18 }
```

Figure 11.2

The what function in the e object on line 14 displays the error message. When executed, the program in Fig. 11.2 displays

```
in catch block
basic_string::erase: __pos (which is 2) > this->size() (which is 1)
after catch block
```

The various types of exception classes form a hierarchy. The exception class is the base class. Thus, it is at the top of the hierarchy. Some of the classes that are derived from exception are bad_cast, logic_error, and runtime_error. One of the classes derived from the logic_error class is the out_of_range class. This is the type of the exception created on line 9 in Fig. 11.2.

The type of the parameter in a catch block determines the type of the exceptions it will catch. Because exception is at the top of the class hierarchy, the catch block in Fig. 11.2 will catch any exception in the class hierarchy. For example, it will catch the out_of_range exception that line 9 throws. This makes sense. Because the out_of_range class inherits everything in the exception class, it is an exception object with some extra stuff in it (inherited from the out_of_range and the logic_error classes). If we change line 11

```
11    catch (exception &e)       // catches any exception
```
                to
```
11    catch (out_of_range &e)    // catches only out_of_range exception
```

the catch block will still catch the exception thrown on line 9 because the type of the exception is compatible with the type of the parameter e. However, it will *not* catch any exception not instantiated from out_of_range or one of its derived classes. Moreover, we would need to include the header file stdexcept. Otherwise, all the classes derived from exception would not be available.

In our next example (Fig. 11.3), the exception is not caught in the function in which it occurs. Instead, it is caught higher up in the call chain. main calls f which in turn calls g. The exception occurs in g, but it is caught in main. When the exception is thrown in g, the exception mechanism starts a search for the end of the active try block. g has no try blocks. Thus, a return to f (the caller of g) is forced. As in a normal return, any local variables or parameters in g are destroyed. Thus, the local variable s in g is destroyed. The search continues in f. Because there are no try blocks in f, f returns to main where on line 20 the active try block ends. The catch block that follows the try block (lines 21 tto 24) then catches the exception. Normal execution continues only after the exception is caught. Thus, line 8 in g and line 13 in f are not executed.

```
 1 // f1103.cpp  Exception propagating up the call chain
 2 #include <iostream>
 3 using namespace std;
 4 void g()
 5 {
 6     string s = "a";
 7     s.erase(2);              // throws exception
 8     cout << "not executed\n";
 9 }
10 void f()
11 {
12     g();
13     cout << "not executed\n";
14 }
15 int main()
16 {
17     try
18     {
19         f();;
20     }
21     catch (exception &e)  // exception caught in main
22     {
23         cout << "in catch block in main\n";
24     }
25     cout << "after catch block" << endl;
26     return 0;
27 }
```

Figure 11.3

When executed, the program in Fig. 11.3 displays

```
in catch block in main
after catch block
```

Our next example (Fig. 11.4) contains two catch blocks. The second catch block (lines 24 to 27) has three dots in its parameter list, which makes it a **universal catch block**. That is, it will catch *any* exception that the preceding catch block does not catch. The type of the e parameter in the first catch block (see line 20) is not compatible with the out_of_range exception thrown on line 7 (the out_of_range class is not derived from the bad_cast class). Thus, the universal catch block catches the exception. Because on line 20 we are using a class derived from `exception`, we have to include the header file `stdexcept` (see line 3).

```cpp
 1 // f1104.cpp  Universal catch block
 2 #include <iostream>
 3 #include <stdexcept>        // needed for access to exception class hierarchy
 4 using namespace std;
 5 void g()
 6 {
 7     string s = "a";         // throws out_of_range exception
 8     s.erase(2);
 9 }
10 void f()
11 {
12     g();
13 }
14 int main()
15 {
16     try
17     {
18         f();;
19     }
20     catch (bad_cast &e)  // does not catch exception
21     {
22         cout << "in bad_cast catch block\n";
23     }
24     catch(...)              // catches any exception not already caught
25     {
26         cout << "in universal catch block\n";
27     }
28     cout << "after catch block\n";
29     return 0;
30 }
```

Figure 11.4

When executed, the program in Fig. 11.4 displays

```
in universal catch block
after catch block
```

throw instruction

In all the exception examples we have seen so far, the problem that generates the exception is detected by the exception mechanism. However, a programmer can include code that checks for possible problems. If a problem is detected, the included code can create and throw an exception for that problem using the `throw` statement. A `catch` block can then catch the exception and take the necessary action to handle the problem. An alternative is to throw an exception but not have a `catch` block, in which case the exception would force the termination of the program. This occurs when the program in Fig. 11.5 is executed. This program prompts the user for a non-negative number. After reading it in, it computes on line 13 the number's square root by calling the `sqrt` function. But before it computes the square root, the program checks on line 11 if the entered number is negative. If it is, it does not have a square root. Thus, in that case the program on line 12 throws an exception that has the effect of terminating the program.

```
1 // f1105.cpp  throw instruction
2 #include <iostream>
3 #include <stdexcept>
4 #include <cmath>
5 using namespace std;
6 int main()
7 {
8     double d;
9     cout << "enter non-neg number\n";
10    cin >> d;
11    if (d < 0.0)
12        throw(invalid_argument("arg must be non-neg"));
13    cout << sqrt(d) << endl;  // executed only if exception not thrown
14    return 0;
15 }
```

Figure 11.5

The type of the exception thrown by line 12 is `invalid_argument`. This class is derived from the `logic_error` class which in turn is derived from the `exception` class. Because the program is using a class in the class hierarchy below the `exception` class, it includes the `stdexcept` header file (see line 3). The `string` constant on line 12 is an error message that will be incorporated into the exception object created by the `throw` instruction. This error message is displayed when the program if forced to terminate. When the program is run, if a non-negative number is entered, the program computes and displays the square root. For example,

```
enter non-negative number
9
3
```

But if a negative number is entered, the program is forced to terminate. But before it does, it displays an error message that includes the `string` constant on line 12. For example,

```
enter
-9
terminate called after throwing an instance of 'std::invalid_argument'
  what():  arg must be non-neg
```

Epilog

Your next step should be to study *C and C++ Under the Hood Second Edition* (same author as this book). It covers most of the features of C++ covered in this book but at the machine/assembly instruction level. It provides the reader with a wonderful insight on how C and C++ work and should clear up any topic in this book that you do not quite understand. It also provides an introduction to microprogramming (programming that defines the machine language of a computer) and systems programming. After that, try *Writing Interpreters and Compilers for the Raspberry Pi Using Python Second Edition*. You do not need a Raspberry Pi computer (a software simulator is provided) or know Python to use this book. After completing this series, you should be well prepared to tackle any subject in applied computer science. Good luck and be well.

AJDR

INDEX